REA

FRIENDS
OF ACPL

DO NOT REMOVE
CARDS FROM POCKET

362.3 M76M
MONTY, SHIRLEE.   7048087
MAY'S BOY :

ALLEN COUNTY PUBLIC LIBRARY

FORT WAYNE, INDIANA 46802

You may return this book to any agency, branch,
or bookmobile of the Allen County Public Library

DEMCO

P9-DGV-329

MAY'S
BOY

MAY'S BOY

An Incredible Story of Love

by
Shirlee Monty

Thomas Nelson Publishers
Nashville

ALLEN COUNTY PUBLIC LIBRARY
FORT WAYNE, INDIANA

Second printing

Copyright © 1981 by Shirlee Monty and May Lemke

All rights reserved. Written permission must be secured from the publisher to use or reproduce any part of this book, except for brief quotations in critical reviews or articles.

Published in Nashville, Tennessee, by Thomas Nelson, Inc., Publishers and distributed in Canada by Lawson Falle, Ltd., Cambridge, Ontario.

Printed in the United States of America.

Cover design by American Motivate.
Cover black-and-white photo *The Milwaukee Journal* by Dale Guldan.

Library of Congress Cataloging in Publication Data

Monty, Shirlee.
  May's boy.

  1. Lemke, Leslie. 2. Mentally handicapped—United States—Biography. I. Title.
RC570.M54   362.3'092'4   [B]   81-14160
ISBN 0-8407-4091-3   AACR2

7048087

This book is lovingly dedicated
to
Leslie Lemke
my nephew Mark Turcin
and
retarded people everywhere.
To their potential, their growth,
and our understanding.

Contents

Acknowledgments

Few books are written alone. Standing in the shadows are those people who give so freely of themselves—offering advice, encouragement, and support when needed.

With these people I wish to share the credit, and to them express my gratitude.

To my husband, Lee, who urged me to write this book and offered valuable suggestions, emotional support, and in so many ways helped make the path easier.

To my four children, Lynn, Joe, Jane, and Anne, whose lively presence and enthusiasm for their own lives so often distracted and refreshed me from the long, lonely hours of writing.

To the editors at Thomas Nelson Publishers, Peter Gillquist, Larry Stone, Bruce Nygren, and Lisa Hemby, who so patiently guided me through this project, and with tact and encouragement helped develop my journalistic approach into a more narrative style.

To Stance Bergelin, Dr. Darold Treffert, Paul Baum-gartener, and John Wilberding, for giving so willingly of their time, insight, and expertise.

To May and Joseph Lemke, who shared so much of their lives, so that ours might be enriched.

And most of all, my gratitude to Jesus Christ, who made it all possible.

MAY'S
BOY

Chapter 1

Who Are the Lemkes?

I don't know why certain people etch themselves in our minds forever, while others slip out of our thoughts without ever leaving a mark.

The first time I met the Lemkes, I knew I would not forget them. They were there to stay, forever in my memories.

I first heard of May, Joe, and Leslie Lemke in July, 1980, when I was in the final stages of a book on the life of Terry Meeuwsen, former Miss America and Milwaukee television personality.

Almost a year earlier, when we had started the book, I had suggested taping at my home in the suburbs rather than at her office in the studio. I thought Terry might like to get away from her desk and enjoy the informality of a home, where we could both curl up on a chair or sofa.

Usually Terry drove across town and I fixed a light lunch, which gave us a chance to share a little of our personal lives before the grueling afternoons of taping.

So what if the phone sometimes rang or one of my girls dashed in with, "I'm sorry, Mom, but I've just *got* to ask you a question!" Often, it was a nice break from the intensive questioning, and we'd both laugh at the breathless urgency of teenaged daughters.

On this particular day, however, Terry didn't breeze in with her usual, "Hi, how's everybody?" Obviously, she had something else on her mind. Before I could say a word, she was halfway through the doorway and had blurted out, "Shirlee, did you see the show this morning?"

"No, I didn't," I confessed. I had been rushing around, fixing lunch, organizing questions, setting up the tape recorder, making sure everything was in order.

Terry continued excitedly, her words tumbling over each other. "I had a guest this morning who was *incredible*. In fact, there were three guests: May, Joseph, and Leslie Lemke. The Lemkes took Leslie in when he was six months old. He was totally helpless—severely handicapped—and May literally devoted the next twenty-eight years of her life to that boy—every minute of the day. She was determined to make something out of him—'to find God's gift for him,' as she put it.

"She told about all the years she had worked and waited for some sign, all the heartbreak she had suffered, and finally, what she called 'the miracle.' That was the night he first played the piano.

"Anyway, we were all crying—the audience, the staff, the cameramen, and me—right on camera! The phones started ringing before the show was even over. The whole thing was just unbelievable!"

I was intrigued. But since I hadn't seen the show and we had other things to talk about, the subject was dropped.

My phone rang the next day. A close friend was calling. Had I seen Terry's show on Friday? Well, there was this incredible lady, May Lemke, and she had this retarded son, Leslie. . . .

Two days later, I received another call. "Shirlee, if you're ever looking for another book project, you ought to contact the Lemkes. Did you see them on Terry's show?"

After a half-dozen more phone calls, I called Terry. "Do you have the Lemkes' phone number? I've got to meet this family. They seem to have created quite a stir!"

I called May, and she said she'd be delighted to see me. Her voice was lively, with a heavy British accent. We set a date for the following Wednesday afternoon.

On Wednesday, I drove twenty miles out to a small town west of Milwaukee, then circled Pewaukee Lake until I spotted a mailbox with JOE LEMKE inscribed in large, black letters. Leaning against the fence, watching for me, was Joe.

He was much older than I had expected, possibly in his late seventies. I began calculating mentally how old he must have been when they took in Leslie. Could he have been fifty? And he took in an infant—a helpless, handicapped baby, at that. Wow! The thought was mind boggling!

I took a good look at his face. He had a gentle expression; his skin was softly lined, crinkles around the eyes, a warm, merry smile. He was dressed like a working man in old worn jeans, a faded flannel shirt, and shoes that were showing the wear. As we walked through the gate, I noticed that he was a trifle stooped, his gait that of a man beginning to feel the years. He looked like a good man—honest, no airs. I liked him at once.

A small yellow cottage sat at the bottom of the hill; beyond, I could see the lake, placid and green. Only a sailboat and a few fishing boats had ventured out on this languid afternoon.

I saw that the Lemkes were not isolated. There were homes on either side of their property and many more scattered around the lake. The lake probably came alive on weekends, but today it was quiet.

"That's where I keep all my tools and chop my wood," Joe said as he pointed to an old basement on our way down the hill. He spoke softly, a bit muffled, and I had to listen carefully in order not to miss a word. He was showing me his tomato plants and flower beds when something flew out the back door, captured me in a bear hug, and abruptly finished whatever Joe was telling me.

Was it a leprechaun? For a moment, I wasn't sure. It turned out to be May Lemke, all four and a half feet and ninety pounds of her.

A trifle reserved myself, I was nearly overcome by this dynamic little Englishwoman, with her blond, curly hair and bright red lipstick, who darted around the yard like an animated teenager.

"We planted all these trees, everything out here. I have lots of pineys in the spring . . ." I saw they were peonies. I had to adjust to the British accent. "And we have a pear tree," she went on, "here, try one. Why, we get two or three bushels, I share them with the neighbors, we share everything, you know. . . ."

My frenetic tour included grapevines, raspberry bushes, some friendly chipmunks (she pointed to the little sign, *Chipmunk Crossing,* and said they always let the chipmunks pass first), more fruit trees, blue spruce, dozens of friendly birds hovering around, maybe waiting for an introduction.

All of a sudden, she stopped in front of a slightly misshapen evergreen tree. "This is Joe Perry," she said. I wondered if some sort of greeting was expected. But she went on.

"You see, Joe Perry used to sell bushes and trees. He was a lovely man, but he's dead now. Anyway, I went in looking for trees, and I found this one in a corner, looking kind of wobbly and out of shape. Joe saw me looking at it pitifully and he said, 'May, I've been telling that tree that someone who really loves trees will come in some day and take care of it,' and I said, 'Well, that's me.'

"So I brought it home and I call it Joe Perry and I talk to it every day. 'Joe Perry,' I say, 'you are really looking lovely today,' and just look at it. It was nothing but a little cripple when I got it, and now it's getting tall and strong and that little hole is filling up real good."

Finally, the tour over, May pulled me into the house to meet Leslie. In the tiny kitchen, I was able to take a closer look at May.

Her face was well lined, dominated by pale green, deepset, rather heavy-lidded eyes. In the months ahead, I discovered that those eyes were a barometer of her feelings. They could flash with anger or sparkle with laughter. They would harden when she talked of the pain and terror of war and then suddenly soften as she spoke of her love of Jesus Christ.

Like Joe, she looked to be in her late seventies, but that's where the similarities between them ended. She was as lively and irrepressible as he was calm and soft-spoken.

"Would you like something to eat? Now, just make yourself at home. Act like you live here. And where are your people from?" My answers couldn't keep pace with her questions.

I looked at my surroundings and saw that beyond the small living room was a narrow, closed-in porch, much of it taken up with an upright piano. Surrounded by other rooms, the living room was rather dimly lit, and I was halfway through before I realized that someone was sitting in a chair.

I turned and there was Leslie, with his head down, hands folded, very still. Had he heard me come in? I reached out to take his hand. When I touched him, his whole body trembled. "Speak to him first," May said, right at my shoulder. "You have to let him know you're there. Then you can touch him or take his hand. But you must do it softly, gently—never abruptly."

"Hello, Leslie," I said. "I'm Shirlee Monty, and I've come to hear you play the piano." (What else would I do wrong? I wasn't sure if he could understand me. I didn't know much about retardation. I had been told that Leslie was severely retarded. What did that mean? Could he understand me? Could he talk?)

I felt a bit uncomfortable, uneasy. Leslie was

obviously very handicapped. When May asked him to go to the porch to play for me, I wondered if I ought to help him. She must have read my thoughts, because she motioned me out of the way.

"Let Leslie go first," she said. "We don't help him. We want him to learn to do things for himself."

So, by holding onto a ledge, a doorknob, the arm of a chair, Leslie managed to feel his way to the piano, his limbs trembling, and with a little more effort, he positioned himself on the bench.

When he first stood up, I had been surprised at how tall he was. I noticed he was several inches taller than Joe—about six feet. I had expected him to be heavy, which so often happens to people who are sedentary. But Leslie was not overweight. He looked as if he weighed about a hundred and fifty pounds.

His eye sockets were a bit sunken, his forehead somewhat prominent, but even though his eyelids were always closed, there was nothing unsightly or unattractive about him. He had a strong, square face and reddish-blond hair, and if anything, looked younger than his twenty-eight years.

"Now, what would you like to hear?" May asked.

"What would I like to hear?" I repeated. "What can he play?"

"He can play anything," May said. "Just ask him."

This must be some kind of a joke, I thought to myself, but May persisted.

"Does he play classical, modern, religious music, or what?" I asked. I noticed that Leslie was not even attempting to talk. "I mean, what is his area?"

"Anything," she repeated.

I decided to go along with it. Funny, I could hardly

think of a song. "Okay," I said, "play 'Everything Is Beautiful.' "

"Yes, yes," Leslie said in a flat, guttural tone. From a slumped position, he straightened his body, lifted his head, and positioned his hands. Suddenly, those spastic fingers flew up and down the keyboard, striking rich, strong chords, interspersed with delicate, running notes—loud, then soft, with perfect timing, never missing a note. A deep, baritone voice filled the room, sending the lyrics resounding throughout the entire house. "Everything is beautiful," he sang, "in its own way."

"Doesn't he have a powerful voice?" May was saying, but I was too preoccupied with Leslie to answer. Thoughts were tumbling all around in my mind in a jumble of confusion. *Where did he learn that song? He can't read music if he can't even see the piano keys. How does he know the keyboard? If he can hardly speak, then how can he sing like that? If he's spastic, how can his fingers find the keys, never missing a note?*

I suddenly felt challenged by this young man. " 'Rhapsody in Blue,' " I offered. The rendition was magnificent. " 'The Entertainer' from *The Sting*." He never missed a note. *Something faster. Let's see, what's really fast?* "Elvis Presley's 'Jail House Rock'." I couldn't even see his fingers on that one. *Something really tough.* "Rachmaninoff's Concerto No. 2 in E Minor." I closed my eyes and mentally drifted off to Carnegie Hall.

The hours flew by as I tested him on more classics, ragtime, rock, ballads, show tunes, old war songs—everything I could think of. Leslie kept flipping them out of some inexhaustible storehouse, some never-ending repertoire.

When I ran out of titles, *he* kept going. I was treated to German waltzes, French cabaret songs, and beautiful Italian arias.

He finally capped his performance that lovely afternoon with two powerful hymns: "How Great Thou Art" and "The Lord's Prayer." That was when my cautious, questioning mind dissolved in a flood of tears. *Who cares where this strange phenomenon comes from?* I said to myself. *Whatever the explanation, it's beautiful!*

I left that afternoon feeling that I had overstayed my welcome, but the Lemkes couldn't have been more gracious. Leslie was obviously a tireless performer.

I told them they would hear from me soon. I needed time to think about what I had seen and heard. I knew I wanted to write about Leslie, but did I have the time immediately to do another book?

Why not start out with the *Milwaukee Journal?* A feature article would be a good test run. I called Jim Cattey, metro editor. I had done assignments for Jim before. He liked the idea and told me to go ahead. I returned to the Lemkes, and the *Journal* sent out a photographer. He came back with one good shot, but he didn't feel it was enough. "We really ought to do an entire layout on this one," he said. "Those people are something else!"

Two weeks later, the Lemkes landed on the front page of the *Journal* with close to a full page spread inside. The story was picked up by the Associated Press and used in newspapers all over the country.

In less than a week, every local television station around Milwaukee presented a segment on the Lemkes and their story of hope and love and faith.

National radio and television shows followed. In less than two months, the Lemkes were featured on "Paul Harvey News," "Walter Cronkite Evening News," "That's Incredible!" and a few months later, "The 700 Club."

The Lemkes had touched a troubled and cynical world, restoring to awareness the fact that love is powerful, perseverance prevails, and Jesus Christ still lives.

Yet viewers were far from satisfied. They wanted to know more about the Lemkes. Who were they? Where did they come from? How had May and Joe persisted in their love for Leslie?

I set out to answer those questions, and I found myself retracing May's steps until we reached the point where it all began: a little village in northern England, almost eighty years ago.

Chapter 2
Beginnings

Dusk in the little fishing village of Monkwear-mouth, England, at the turn of the century . . . The smell of fish and chips permeates the night air as villagers slowly make their way to the open-air stalls, where vendors are cooking the day's catch, fresh cod, dipped in batter and fried in oil. Another community pot of oil is sizzling with thickly sliced potatoes.

"Middle or tail?" the vendors call out. Some customers like the thick, fleshy part of the fish while others prefer the crunchiness of the tail. The steaming pieces of cod and potatoes are wrapped in newspaper and exchanged for threepence.

Meanwhile, children hustle to the pub on the corner with empty jugs, to bring back robust ale for their fathers. Finally, everything is ready at home: salt and vinegar for the fish, hot tea for the women and children.

Such was the nightly ritual of the sturdy Englishmen of Monkwearmouth, who worked from sunup to twilight on the boats or in the mines. Fish and chips, plenty of ale, and the family crowded close to the fire.

Later in the evening, the men drifted to the pubs for a quiet draught of ale, silently puffing their pipes until closing time.

On one of those typical nights, Samuel Hansen came running out of his house, calling for a midwife. "She's started! She's started!" he shouted. Everyone knew that Maria Hansen was expecting her seventh child. Mr. Hansen ran to the home of one of the women who knew how to deliver babies and pulled her out of her house, down the narrow street, and through his own door.

He was back outside in less than an hour. There was a bit of a swagger in his walk now. Pride had replaced concern. "Another girl," he announced to his neighbors who had gathered outside. "We're callin' her May."

The peculiar name *Monkwearmouth* is derived from the location of the village. It is situated near a centuries-old monastery on the northern mouth of the Wear River.

At the southern mouth of the river lies Sunderland, a shipping port as well as a shipbuilding and coal-mining center. The Wear empties into the North Sea, a body of water about the size of Texas with a shore line of four thousand miles. To this day, much of the eastern seaboard of England and Scotland is devoted to the fishing industry.

Fog moves in almost daily in this region, and the sea keeps the weather moderately cool year-round.

Icebergs loom to the north, giving the massive black waters an eerie, desolate look. Sometimes you can almost hear the cries of the people who have gone down in that sea.

Monkwearmouth is a very, very old village, reputed to have been built by the Romans. Stone houses line the cobblestone streets, and after a rain, everything is clean and glistening, the white stones sparkling in the sunlight. But when the fog rolls in, the village takes on an almost opaque look, gray and hazy in the mist.

In the early 1900s, almost everything in the village was built from stone—the steps to the houses, the huge fireplaces, the long cooking tables, the floors. There were even scouring stones to clean and polish the tables and steps to a bright, translucent finish. Only the inside stairs and second floor were made of wood.

The daily life of the people was as routine and predictable as their evening fish and chips. The village began to come alive at three or four in the morning, when the "knocker-uppers" arrived with their long poles. For a few pennies a week, they awakened the villagers by tapping on their bedroom windows. The tap-tap-tapping sounds could be heard faintly throughout the village as the knocker-uppers moved from house to house, alerting the drowsy occupants that morning was nigh.

Soon less gentle sounds echoed through the streets. Coal miners' heavy boots made loud clanking sounds on the cobblestones as they trudged off to their underground caves. Later came the hurried footsteps of fishermen, shipbuilders, and butchers, off to begin their day's work. Shortly afterwards, the children skipped off to another day at school, then housewives came bustling or sent their small children scurrying at the first sign of the milk carts jolting awkwardly over the cobblestones.

"How much milk today?" the vendor asked at each house. "A pint or a quart?" Then he carefully ladled one portion as the child or mother held out an empty jug. "Any eggs? Butter? Cheese?" The subtle fragrance of fresh cheeses and creamy butter drifted through the air.

More wagons clattered over the cobblestones—some loaded with cod, others heaped with produce. Women hurried out of their kitchens with the day's order. "Heads on today, dearie, to make soup. Nay, not that one, yer silly bloke. G'wan. I want a middle to it!" Later, in the market, the wives rummaged through the vegetables for the largest cabbage, the longest carrots, the freshest brussels sprouts.

At the end of the week, they walked to the butcher's to buy beef, lamb, kidneys, or rabbit. Although fish and chips were the weekly staple, the Sunday dinner might be steak and kidney pie, boiled rabbit, shepherd's pie, or roast beef with Yorkshire pudding.

Most of the work at home centered around the fireplace, with its large iron ovens on either side. The first tantalizing odors of the day came from these ovens as breads were baked to perfection. On Sundays, the aroma of rabbit or the day's stew permeated the kitchen as dinner was set to simmer in the large iron kettle that hung from a bar directly over the coals. Another huge pot sat on the fire for boiling clothes. Next to the oven was a small basin for washing up. On days the floor had to be swilled, the hot soapy water that had been used for clothes was poured on the floor and the stones scrubbed with stiff brushes.

Life was hard work; the simple chores of survival—cooking, cleaning, and gathering food into the house—were enough to keep a household busy from dawn to dusk.

Samuel Hansen was a big man, a shipbuilder by trade, and he wasn't home much to see his ten children grow up. The royal service sent him all over the world, often for months at a time.

But when he was home, he always found his curious little daughter May waiting with plenty of questions. He loved this lively child with the curly, golden hair and the wide, greenish-brown eyes. She wasn't a chatterbox like the three younger girls, but she was inquisitive, fascinated with everything around her.

"Daddy," she began on one of his rare trips home, "everybody in our family is big except me. Why am I so small?"

Samuel put his hand on his daughter's head and said gently, "May, dear, don't you ever worry about being small. You have a quick brain and a good sense of humor, so wherever you go, you'll get along fine."

Maria Hansen was a serious woman, very kind and gentle. A nurse and midwife, she often was called away from home to deliver a baby. Sometimes her patient would be only down the street, and the children would listen for the first cries of the new arrival. "Mama will be home soon," May would say. "I can hear the baby crying!" Mrs. Hansen must have brought a hundred babies into the world; not once did she ask a fee.

Like many of her neighbors, Mrs. Hansen was an expert on herbs and home remedies. She gave her children a dose of sweet spirits of niter when they were sick and applied a paste of slippery elm bark for rashes, sores, and wounds. Eating parsley was supposed to break up kidney stones.

Whiskey or brandy was poured over wounds as an antiseptic. Sweet oil was a staple in every medicine cabinet, for it was rubbed liberally on arms, legs, shoulders, and chests anytime there were aches and pains or fevers. Children received cod liver oil or a mixture of cod liver oil and malt from the time they were babies.

But if they were very ill, they were taken to the infirmary for medication or injections. Infirmaries, as well as hospitals, were financed by the government, so that all examinations, operations, medications, and services were free.

Bedtime at the Hansen home began with stories, most often about Jesus, and ended with music: hymns, English folk songs, and the children's favorite, "Ten Little Indians."

May's prized possession for many years was the rag doll her mother had made for her when she was just two. She carried the doll everywhere, including to meals, where she kept up a constant conversation with her "child." "Now, mind your manners. Stay clean and neat whilst you eat!" When one of her brothers accidentally sat on the doll one morning, May spent the rest of the day nursing it back to health.

Beggars frequently knocked on the door of the Hansen home, knowing that the kindly Mrs. Hansen always would offer them a sandwich and a cup of hot tea. How often her children heard her say, "If someone knocks on your door, don't turn him away. You never know who it's going to be!"

Music was the home entertainment in those days, and in the evenings music often came through the windows of the Hansen home. Maria might be cradling a new baby in her arms, singing a soft lullaby. Sometimes the family played the gramophone that Samuel Hansen had brought home to his wife. Maria played Caruso records until they wore out.

When May was older, she played the piano, singing at the top of her voice, "I'll Take You Home Again, Kathleen" (her father's favorite). Whoever the performer, one thing was certain: Those Hansens loved music!

Young men and women left home early to marry, the custom in England in the early 1900s. They were frequently "traded off," which meant their parents selected a husband or wife for them. Somewhere around the age of twelve, children were expected either to marry or to support themselves with a trade. By the time a girl had a menstrual cycle, she was deemed old enough for wedlock. One of May's sisters was married at twelve, and all the Hansen boys left at that age to go out and earn a living—all except one.

When May was not quite two years old, her oldest brother, not yet twelve, was already out learning a trade. He came home early one day, looking pale and strange around the mouth.

"Are you all right, Snowball?" Mrs. Hansen asked. The family called him Snowball because of his beautiful, golden hair. May ran to her mother and held onto her mother's skirts, which she always did when Maria looked worried.

Snowball said he didn't feel well.

"I just made a rabbit pie, dear," Mrs. Hansen said. "Come and eat. Then you can go to bed."

"I don't feel like eating, Mama. I'm so tired."

"All right. If you don't feel well, I'll help you up to bed."

He really seems quite ill, Maria thought to herself. *I'll take him to my own room, where he can rest on the big bed.* Still clinging to her skirts, May followed her mother into the big bedroom with the large oak bed and the beautiful valance that her father had made. She loved this room with her mama's patchwork quilt and the frills all around the bottom of the bed. When one of the children was very ill, Maria Hansen always brought him into her bedroom.

But now May was distracted. "Why is Snowball so tired? Is he sick?" she kept asking again and again. Too preoccupied to answer, Maria carefully turned down the covers, plumped up the pillows, and gently helped her son into the bed.

In a very faint voice Snowball asked, "Mother, would you put your arm around my neck? Pull me up a little bit."

As she lifted her son, blood flowed out of his mouth in a gush and ran all over the bed. Mrs. Hansen screamed, then called out, "Oh, William! Oh, William!" He died in her arms.

Coming home from work that day, Snowball had

stopped to help a friend move a sewing machine up a long, narrow flight of stairs. When they nearly reached the top, Snowball slipped. The heavy machine struck him, and machine and boy fell all the way down the steps.

May's sunny disposition was a comfort after William died and soon made her a favorite with her mother—as well as with everyone who knew her. She seemed to sense when to be funny and when to be serious, an unusual trait in a child so young. Maria Hansen called her "my little ray of gold."

Because of her curiosity, May became an explorer almost as soon as she could walk. The first time she disappeared, she was just three years old. Mrs. Hansen knocked on every door, looking for her little girl. She was searching the streets when at last she found her, walking along with a blind man.

Sensing that Mrs. Hansen was upset, the man asked how old her daughter was. "She's only three," Mrs. Hansen answered.

"Only three?" he remarked. "Well, she's quite a little girl. She's taken me to every house and sold all my laces for me!"

"God must be with that child," Maria Hansen often said. "She goes investigating everywhere, but He always brings her home."

May was four when she wandered into the Jewish colony on one of her journeys. In Monkwearmouth, the Jewish people lived in a segregated area that the Gentiles normally didn't visit. She was intrigued by this new territory, so she walked the lanes and looked around. The Jewish mothers were outside nursing their babies, and May sat down to watch for a while. They told her how the first milk from the mother's breasts was used to wash out the baby's eyes.

"Did they do that to my eyes?" May asked.

"I think they did, but you'll have to ask your Mama," she was told.

After a while, May walked on. She climbed some steps, looked through a window, and saw a man with a black hat standing at the head of a long table full of children. The group looked as if they were praying. May knocked on the door, and the man invited her to eat with them.

All the children were very friendly, and they chatted amiably during the delicious dinner. Some of the dishes tasted strange to May, but she was too polite not to eat everything. When they had finished their meal, the man kindly suggested that May go home— her mother most likely would be worried. But before May left, he gave her what looked like a stack of large cookies to take home to her mother. She thanked the man, said good-bye to the children, and started home.

When May walked in the door, she saw at once that her mother was worried. "May, I've been looking all over for you," she scolded. "I've been up and down the street knocking on every door. Where have you been this time?"

"But, Mama," May said excitedly, "see what I brought you. Some beautiful cookies!" She handed the parcel to her mother.

Mrs. Hansen's face softened, and then she smiled. "Now I know where you were, my little wanderer.

You were in the Jewish colony. Those aren't cookies, May. They're Passover cakes. Come. We'll spread butter on them, and they'll be delicious!"

May earned her nickname "The Searcher" from a priest, when she ended up in his church on one of her excursions. She had gone into the church by herself and was kneeling in one of the pews when he saw her. He walked over and put his hand on her head.

"Hello, there. It looks like you came to pay us a visit," he said, smiling down at her. "Did you know I have a name for little visitors like you? I call them 'the searchers.' "

Then he took her by the hand and led her to the street. "And where do you live, my little friend?" May pointed in the direction of her house.

"I'll take you there," he said. With all the courtesy of a gentleman, he escorted the little girl home. "Remember now," he remarked as he left her at the door. "You are called a searcher!"

Another time when May was out walking, this time with her mother, she saw a horse with a broken leg lying in the street. Immediately she ran over, slid to her knees, and lifted the horse's head into her lap. People were already gathering around. Bobbies had arrived to keep order until someone could come to put the animal to sleep.

One of the bobbies asked Mrs. Hansen to take her daughter away. "She will never leave that horse," May's mother replied. "May will try to make him stand if she can. Perhaps you can explain the situation to her."

Nodding his head, the bobby walked over to May

and spoke from his lofty height. "It's very sad, child, but this horse has broken his leg and can never walk again. We'd like to help him, but there's nothing we can do. We'll have to put him to sleep. The horse won't suffer that way. Now, perhaps you'd better run along with your Mum."

May listened very thoughtfully. Then resolutely she stood up, said good-bye to the horse, and mother and daughter walked silently home.

Children in Monkwearmouth didn't decorate Christmas trees or enjoy visits from Santa Claus, but they did get "goodies" on Christmas Eve. Their mothers made aprons, large and roomy, and on Christmas Eve the children could go out begging. Custom mandated that the children be five years of age or younger to beg, and they were allowed to go to only one house.

They knocked on the door, and when it opened, they sang:

> *I wish you a Merry Christmas*
> *And a Happy New Year.*
> *We are teetotalers*
> *And we don't drink beer.*
> *A little bit of spice cake,*
> *A little bit of cheese.*
> *A glass of cold water or*
> *A penny if you please.*
> *And if you haven't a penny,*
> *A farthing will do.*
> *And if you haven't a farthing,*
> *Well, God bless you.*

Then they held out their aprons to be filled with apples, oranges, pears, nuts, candy, pieces of cake, and sometimes, even a farthing (a quarter of a penny).

Monks from the nearby monastery walked through the village streets on holidays and holy days, carrying lighted candles. May was fascinated by their long, flowing robes, and it was not at all unusual to see the tiny girl walking alongside them, asking if she could carry a candle, too.

School began early for these English youngsters. They started in at the age of three and usually were finished with their formal education by age twelve. Discipline was severe. May was only three years old when she was punished for jumping up and crying out to go to the water closet. For this unruly behavior, she was rapped on the hand with a ruler so hard that a small bone was broken. Her father went to school to express his anger, but his remarks carried little weight.

Besides learning reading, writing, and arithmetic, the boys were introduced to trades, while the girls were taught the rudiments of housekeeping: mending, cooking, cleaning, and needlework.

May was six or seven when her teacher announced that they would take up baking. Mrs. Hansen made May some white elasticized sleeves to cover her arms and a little white apron and cap. And May's teacher soon sent the child home with two small loaves of bread, one white and one brown. "Take these to your mother, May, and show her what fine work you've done for y'self."

When the boys and girls were twelve, they were given certificates, their entry card into the working world. The certificates confirmed that they had passed their examinations and were of good character and of sound health.

Most children began their working lives as servants in rich households. From there, they advanced in the areas to which they were suited. Boys became footmen, chauffeurs, bootblacks, gardeners, and butlers, while the girls learned to be maids, cooks, and nurse-governesses.

But many of May's generation would never find their way to their appointed trade. Ominous warnings had been in the air for months. Almost certainly, England would go to war.

Chapter 3

The Cruel, Cruel War

Beginning in the late nineteenth century, tensions among the European powers led to increased militarism, the buildup of arms, and the development of new weapons. By 1907, the six great European powers had squared off into two armed camps: the triple Alliance of Germany, Italy, and Austria-Hungary and the Triple Entente of Great Britain, France, and Russia. The international situation was so volatile by 1914 that Wilhelm von Schön, German ambassador to France, remarked, "Peace remains at the mercy of an accident."

The accident occurred on June 28 of that year, when Archduke Francis Ferdinand, heir to the throne of Austria-Hungary, was assassinated by a Serbian nationalist. As a result, Germany, the greatest military power in Europe, declared war on Serbia, then Russia, and finally France. The most bloody and costly war in modern history to that time had begun.

England entered the war on August 4, 1914, after

Belgian neutrality was violated. It was 1915 before enough men could be recruited to wage an all-out battle.

Much of World War I involved trench warfare and hand-to-hand combat between the largest armies ever seen up to that time. Eventually, six hundred miles of trenches stretched across France and Belgium. Huge underground caverns served as first-aid stations, supply centers, and living quarters for the troops.

The Germans developed dirigibles, or blimps, as part of their Air Force and used them to bomb London in 1915. In 1916, the British army first used the tank. Other new, mechanized vehicles—trucks, automobiles, and motorcycles—accelerated the war on land. For the first time, airplanes and airships bombed soldiers and civilians. Submarines torpedoed merchant ships without warning.

On April 22, 1915, Germany unleashed a new weapon in its drive to the French coast: chlorine gas. French troops fled as the poisonous, greenish-white mist drifted toward them and stung their eyes and throats. Into this massacre, England sent her finest men.

May Hansen lost her father, her four brothers, and most of her uncles, male cousins and friends in the war. One by one, they all were killed.

Maria Hansen cried many times in those four years. Whenever she raised her white apron to her face, May always knew what was wrong. Even though she was older now (almost twelve) she still reverted to her old habit. Quietly, she went to her mother and held onto her dress.

Boys fourteen and fifteen years old, who had never held a gun before, went off to war. Their mothers, using what little food they had—usually biscuits and tea—gave farewell parties for them.

Mrs. Hansen always put a dash of rum in the tea to give the boys courage for where they were going. Then she said, "Go on now, children. Enjoy each other. Sing, dance, and be happy." She knew this might be their last chance to be together. "They'll be gun fodder when they get to France," she told May. She was right. Not one of them ever came back.

When May's Uncle Bill had to leave, he took her in his arms and said, "May, dear, this is good-bye. Your Uncle Billy has to go." He was killed two weeks later.

Maria tried to explain his death to the children. "It's horrible," she said. "They use mustard gas. It rolls on the ground and goes right into the trenches. The gas burns the men all over, and they come out looking like a roasted piece of meat. Oh, it's terrible!" And she began to sob all over again.

Shortly afterwards Maria received news of her husband's death. This time she could hardly speak about what had happened. "Children," she said between sobs, "your father died today. He died a horrible death. They said he'd been in the sea for days and days, and he was just dead rotten. They're bringing him home to be buried in a closed coffin, so none of you can look at him. That's all I can tell you."

May noticed that with all the sorrow, her mother was beginning to waste away. But Maria still tried to comfort her friends, who arrived almost daily, distraught over another death. "Oh, Maria, do you have a little drop of rum?" they asked, and although Maria was no drinker, she always put a few drops of rum in their tea. Her children, too, often came to her upset and crying about the war. Maria always stopped whatever she was doing and said, "Come, love, let's have a cup of tea and talk about what's bothering ya'."

One day when May and her friends were kissing the young boy soldiers good-bye, one lad, crying, said to May, "I have to go to France, but I don't want to leave England." And he clung to her.

May had never seen him before, but she hugged him anyway and said, "Maybe you'll be all right. Remember, you're fighting for England, like we all are."

"But I don't even have a mother to say good-bye to," he protested.

May thought for a moment. "Then why not say good-bye to my mother? She'll cuddle you."

Mrs. Hansen took the boy in her arms, and he sobbed. "Good-bye, son," she said gently. "Of course, you'll come back."

Before England entered the war, Maria Hansen, anticipating the worst, began to put a bit of strawberry jam in a large stone jar every day. She covered and sealed it with rice paper so it wouldn't spoil. The children always wondered what it was for.

Later, when supply ships were being sunk and no food was coming in, she lined up May and her three younger sisters and said, "You were always wondering why I did this. I knew things were going to be bad. There's no food for us now, so this teaspoon of jam will be your meal for today. It will get you by."

Mrs. Hansen had another method for warding off hunger. She told her children to pick up a fresh piece of tar in the street and to chew on it. She said it would keep their teeth nice and lessen the pain of hunger.

So the children chewed tar, and it helped—some.

Everyone was always hungry in the early days of the war. In fact, when the Americans arrived in England in 1917, people were literally starving to death. They could not even take advantage of the ocean's fare because of the bombing and the burning debris on the water. Children were going through garbage, eating anything.

Today May still remembers one poignant time when her prayers for food were answered. If she ever writes a book, she says, it will be called *My Loaf of Bread*.

At one point during the war, word had circulated that a large supply of flour had come in. The bakers went straight to work again, and the people were instructed to line up the following morning. Each family was allotted one loaf.

Mrs. Hansen was helping with the wounded every day, so she told May to pick up their ration. "But go early," she said. "Then you won't have to wait so long."

When May arrived at the distribution center at a little past five the next morning, a long line had already formed. She finally reached the counter late that morning. May received not only a big, beautiful loaf of bread, but an egg and a quarter pound of butter as well.

She couldn't wait to get home to show her mother. As she left, the lady behind the counter cautioned her, "Remember, this is for you to take home. Don't eat any of it on the way, for it must last your family at least a week."

May could hardly keep her promise to get home without eating that loaf of bread. "It smelled so delicious," she told her mother later. "The aroma tormented me every step of the way. I kept saying to myself that I mustn't touch it, but I was craving to get at it." When she finally arrived home, she nearly collapsed from hunger.

May laid the bread on the table, and her mother said, "Well, you've certainly earned something, standing there all that time."

Mrs. Hansen put some butter on a dish, while May prayed silently that she would get the crust. Her mother must have heard, because she cut off a big piece of crust, covered it with butter, and handed it to May. Then she cut herself a thick slice and wrapped the rest for when the other children came in from playing. By then the tea was ready and she poured two big cups of hot tea. The two of them sat together and ate their slices of bread very, very slowly, relishing each bite. Tasting that bread was to become one of the most precious moments of May's childhood.

The war raged on. There was a shortage of everything. Along with food, wood and coal became more and more scarce. May watched in shock as her mother chopped up some of their furniture to build a fire to keep them warm.

Stories came home regularly about the war and the atrocities committed by the Germans. But life on the home front was violent, too. Dirigibles flew overhead, dropping bombs and toppling buildings. Sometimes the crafts would drop low to the ground, and the pilot would shoot tracer bullets through the people below. No matter how fast the victims ran, there was no way of escaping.

Once May and her mother saw a zeppelin explode in the air, scattering German soldiers in all directions. "Oh, Mama, this is terrible!" May cried.

"We must weep for them, too," Mrs. Hansen said. "We all suffer, even the enemy."

Air raid sirens constantly sent people fleeing to their basements or to shelters, where they waited, sometimes all night, for the "all clear" signal.

The people of Monkwearmouth watched ships sink right in front of their eyes. Often they said good-bye to their loved ones as they boarded a vessel in the morning, and by day's end, they were weeping as they watched the ship go down.

Sometimes they looked out over the beach to see hands and feet that had drifted in with the tide; sometimes whole bodies were washed ashore.

On August 6, 1917, the United States declared war on Germany. The British people wept for joy as the Yanks arrived and marched through the streets singing, ". . . and we won't be back till it's over, over there."

The Americans also brought food. One of the first shipments to reach Monkwearmouth was American cheese. The four Hansen girls ate and ate, but they could not get their fill. Finally, Mrs. Hansen cried, "If you children don't stop eating cheese, you're all going to turn yellow!"

The Hansen home, like many English homes, became a gathering place for American soldiers. May's mother nursed the wounded, shared the little food they had, and tried to add a bit of fun to these soldiers' lives before they crossed to the Continent.

One young man who often came to the Hansen

home was a gunrunner from northern Wisconsin named James Pollard. He was a big man, six feet tall and weighing two hundred and forty pounds. Mrs. Hansen loved to hear him describe America and his way of life on a dairy farm. She had a special, motherly feeling for this serious and intense young American.

She learned to love all these Yanks, who were so lonely and far from home. They came to the Hansen home to dance and sing around the piano, trying to forget the war for a few hours. But nobody forgot it for long. The next morning, when Maria Hansen saw a group of soldiers on the beach, looking cold and miserable, she'd say, "Well, I can at least make a pot of tea for those poor fellows. A drink of hot tea is better than nothing."

One of the most heart-wrenching aspects of the war for Maria Hansen was watching lovely, innocent children suffer and die. As the war raged on, more and more English children were orphaned and had nowhere to go. They became beggars and scavengers, wandering the streets.

Often the heads of these precious children were crawling with lice and their clothes were torn and dirty. Whenever Mrs. Hansen saw such neglected youngsters, she gathered them up, brought them in the house, boiled some kind of liquid that killed lice, and cleaned them all up.

As bad as things were, Mrs. Hansen always was able to cheer up her family with a funny story. One such story took place on a morning when she had to go thirty miles away to help with the wounded. While she was in this strange place, the area was bombed and everyone had to go underground. The closest place for safety was an open cellar, so Mrs. Hansen and another lady ran down to wait for the all clear signal.

They kept watch silently through the dark, cold night. Finally, the next morning, the siren sounded. All of a sudden, something ran past the two women like a streak of lightning. They both glimpsed enough to see that it was a naked man. "Just think," Mrs. Hansen told her children, laughing, "we spent the whole night in a cellar with a naked man and didn't even know it!"

As the war progressed, England lost more and more men. Soon everyone was called into the effort, even the children. May was about fourteen when she began working in one of the munitions buildings, first assembling bags of TNT and later filling shells with explosives. Then, a year later, she was assigned to the task of pushing a small trolley loaded with sixty-pound shells to the loading dock. There they were transferred to large trucks.

Food was still very scarce at that time, but the munitions workers were given something each day, usually a sandwich and lemon water to drink. May often wrapped part of her sandwich and took it home to her mother, that sense of kindness and love for others continuing to grow in her.

The ritual was the same every day. May asked, handing her mother the sandwich, "Mama, do you have any tea to drink?"

"No, not today, dear."

Then May took some tea leaves out of her shoe and said, "Well, I sneaked some for you, Mama!"

Mrs. Hansen always smiled and brushed off the leaves, then together they sat and drank their tea,

May watching her mother enjoy her only nourish-
ment of the day. May's mother used the same tea
leaves for a week, scalding them over and over again.

An atmosphere of melancholy prevailed at the
munitions factory, for most of the girls were older
than May and had boyfriends or husbands fighting in
France. May was always trying to cheer them up by
laughing, singing, and dancing. On one of those days
when she had everybody laughing and singing,
May's bright little world collapsed.

The girls had finished loading a trolley, and May
was starting to push it away. They were singing:
"There's a long, long trail a-winding, into the land of
my dreams." On the word *dreams*, there was a
deafening roar. The trolley blew up, throwing fiery
fragments of explosives in every direction.

Suddenly the whole area was engulfed in flames
and screams. People were thrown against walls and
machinery. Buildings exploded. The bursting and
crackling of fire and explosives were everywhere.
Then at last the destruction was done, and new
sounds began: the wails of survivors.

May Hansen was a survivor. She had been thrown
thirty feet against the corner of a building. When they
found her, she was unconscious and badly burned.
The one hundred fifty girls who had been working
outside the building were badly injured or maimed.
The girls inside, all one hundred fifty of them, were
killed.

The entire area was a shambles after the explosion.
Nothing was recognizable. Bodies were found in
fields as far as a quarter mile away. The area had been
hidden and thought to be safe. The trucks were
camouflaged, and the buildings situated very low,

partially underground. Authorities later concluded a spy had tampered with the fuses on the trolley, causing the explosion.

In the hospital May drifted in and out of consciousness for many months. Her mother came to visit, but May rarely recognized her. She only stared at the pretty bouquets of violets and wild flowers that her mother brought, with little understanding of what was happening.

She experienced shooting, searing pain—agony beyond anything she had ever known. Bandages covered almost all of her small frame, with tiny slits to expose her eyes. Tubes ran in and out of her body, and every tooth was missing. Her mother told May later that when she was found after the explosion her mouth was full of TNT.

All of her hair was burned off. One foot was badly burned; it never did resume its normal shape. Her jawbone was broken. An enormous amount of surgery was needed to restore her disfigured face. Her thyroid gland was damaged, and she never grew again after the accident.

May was terrified whenever the nurses came to change her bandages. She began screaming as soon as she heard the sound of their footsteps coming down the hall. The bandages stuck to her burns, and some of the tired, overworked nurses just ripped them off, leaving the little girl bleeding and sobbing helplessly. Somehow, instead of becoming embittered, May grew even more patient, more compassionate, from these harsh experiences.

Finally the burns began to heal, and the pain subsided. May Hansen knew she would make it.

The day arrived when May began the long process

of learning to walk again, this time on crippled feet and legs. She joined with other girls in the hospital who were missing legs and arms. Together they tried to find the courage and strength to overcome their losses and to get on with their lives.

As soon as she was able, May shuffled daily to the infirmary, which was located outside the hospital. There she received two injections daily for pain, one in each arm. Her stoic attitude and cheerful disposition soon made her a favorite with the nuns.

"To think she walks all the way down here, lifts up her little arms, and never cries," one of the sisters said one day. Then she handed May a coin. "Here is a nice golden penny for being such a darling." May limped back to the hospital, clutching the penny and feeling very, very rich.

People at the hospital were kind to little May, knowing she was fighting a huge battle with herself. They knew she was terrified at the thought of facing the world crippled and disfigured.

Often they saw her praying by herself, talking to Jesus. They did what they could to give her courage for her life ahead, wondering if she would ever ask, "Why?"

When her bandages came off, May quickly took up the habit of covering her face with her hands. Her doctor, noticing this, sat down with her one day. "May, dear," he said, "I don't want you ever to cover your face again. Let people see what you look like. You aren't to blame for what happened. You must go out and face the world. Don't ever hide from it. Always look out at the world."

Not long after that talk, May was ready to leave the

hospital. Her doctor hugged her when she left and repeated his admonition. "Now remember, May, don't be afraid. You have courage. You're going to be all right."

When people stared at her or when children teased her and called her "Scarface," May remembered what her doctor had said. She would not hide her face. She would look out at the world. His words gave her the courage to go on.

Maria Hansen was a great comfort to her daughter. She cradled her in her arms and sang to her and tried to encourage her. "No one on earth can protect you, my dear. And there is nothing more that anybody can do for you. Now, it's up to you. May, you are cheerful and clever, and you have such a funny sense of humor. People will always love you."

After four long years the battering of England was over. On November 11, 1918, the fighting was ordered stopped on all battlefronts. The armistice was signed.

The war had been costly in terms of human lives—8,300,000—and in terms of dollars—337 billion. England alone lost nearly a million men.

But for May Hansen the battle was just beginning. The time had come to go out and face her world.

Chapter 4

Nurse May

Although May's education was interrupted by the war years and her stay in the hospital, she had begun training as a nurse-governess when she was twelve years old. "Now you must go to work," her mother had said. "It's up to you."

A nurse-governess differed from a "nanny" in that she was trained in nursing as well as child care. However, both occupations were held in high esteem, and women in those positions often left a lasting impression on the mind and character of their young charges. Winston Churchill wrote of his nanny: "Mrs. Everest it was who looked after me and tended all my wants. It was to her I poured out my many troubles." A high-ranking British naval officer once confided that, faced with an unexpected crisis, he usually asked himself, "What would Nanny do?"

The training was extensive and took several years before completion. The young ladies learned all about childbirth and child care by working under an experienced nurse. They first watched, then assisted at an actual birth, and learned to make formula and to care for babies.

May's initial on-the-job experience was at the home of a lady who was about to deliver her first child. The training nurse already had told May about labor, the process of birth, and exactly how to help during delivery. Since the expectant mother was not to deliver for several days, the nurse decided to take an afternoon off, leaving May alone with her.

As might be expected, a few hours later the woman began labor. Her husband rushed out to get an experienced midwife, and twelve-year-old May was suddenly in charge. May tried to remember what the nurse had taught her. *Let's see,* she thought to herself. *Oh, yes—get two big towels and tie them to the foot rail.* She looked around, found two towels, tied them to the posts, and gave the other ends to the lady.

"Now, pull on the towels when the pains come," May instructed somberly. "Don't cry, milady. It will soon be over. You hang on to your towels, now, and pull very hard. Pull! *Pull!*"

May stood at the foot of the bed, trying to act very experienced, but inside she was terrified. What if the midwife didn't get there in time? What would she do?

Just then she saw the baby's head, and simultaneously she heard voices. The door opened. "It's coming! *It's coming!*" May screamed. The midwife hurried over to guide the baby's head.

After the birth the midwife washed the baby in oil and laid him beside his mother. "Now then," she said to May. "You did a fine job, child. You'll make a splendid nurse-governess. You think very quickly!"

The lady's husband handed May a one-pound note. May could not believe her eyes! A pound note was worth twenty shillings, and a nurse-governess only earned about seven shillings (two dollars) a week. It was like getting a three-week salary!

Nurse-governesses are trained to be creative and are encouraged to use their own ideas. New situations come up all the time. Sharp thinking and immediate solutions are required. During their training, they often are asked how they would handle a particular problem.

May was still young and in training when she recognized such a problem and quickly used her head. A shoe vender came to visit her employer. He brought along some samples and warned his customer at length about how bootblacks often stain shoes and ruin them. Bootblacks were in the employ of most wealthy English homes at that time. Their primary function was to polish shoes and make sure they were in good condition.

"Where may I put these samples so your bootblack won't disturb them?" the vendor asked.

"Nurse May," her employer called. "Take these shoes to your room. They'll be safe there." Obediently May took them away, but as she was turning to leave her room, she looked at the shoes once more.

They certainly do need a polishing, she thought to herself. *What will make them shine without staining them?* An idea popped into her head. *Why not face cream?*

She tiptoed into the lady of the house's boudoir and found some face cream. Safe in her quarters again, she put just a bit of the cream on one of the shoes, then rubbed it off. The shoe looked beautiful, bright and shiny. So she covered all the shoes with cream and buffed them with a sock. The result was a gleaming finish.

When Milady came after the shoes, she asked, "Nurse, who cleaned the gentleman's shoes?"

"I did," May answered.

"Well, I hope he's not cross with you," the Lady said. In a few minutes she returned to tell May that the shoe vendor wished to speak with her.

A bit frightened, May went downstairs. *He doesn't look too angry,* she thought to herself.

"What did you put on those shoes?" he asked.

"You won't laugh at me, will you, sir?"

"No, I won't laugh at you." He smiled down at her. "They're lovely."

She held her breath. *He'll certainly think I'm crazy,* she thought. Then as fast as she could she said, "I used face cream."

His head flew back in gales of laughter. "Face cream? I never would've guessed it! Face cream! Well, yer a pretty clever nurse, after all. 'Ere's a pound note for yer secret. But ye've got to keep it to yer'self."

Eventually May's training was complete, and she went out on her own as a nurse-governess. Wherever she was employed, she was given total responsibility for the children for the first three years of their life. After that they were placed with a tutor to begin their formal education.

Often May began her employ when her charge was an infant; sometimes even before the child was born. The basic needs and training of the child were up to May. For instance, the British practice was to begin toilet training children from infancy. After the baby was fed each time, May spread a large towel on her lap, took up a tiny pot, and put the baby on it. This was also done at regular intervals during the day, until the baby was completely trained.

Manners had to be impeccable. Thus, another important responsibility was to teach the child to eat properly and to behave quietly and politely at the table. Children from families of the upper social classes were also taught the art of side-feeding, which meant learning to take food from the butler or maid and transfer it to their own plate.

May used example, humor, and praise to motivate her young charges. "Why, Mary, how beautifully you hold your fork."

"Charles, your mother will be proud of you."

"What a lovely party we're having today."

Her work was not always easy. The children could be challenging and unpredictable. One such time came during an evening meal. A new employee had been hired, a black butler, and three-year-old Mary kept staring at him quizzically. When he began to serve her pudding, she looked up at him and asked, "Sir, is the pudding black, too?"

"No, no, dear," said May. "It's only him that's black. It's like we say in our prayers, 'Black, white, bond, free, we're all God's children.' He's one of God's children."

Another duty of the nurse-governess was to accompany the children at social events or when the family traveled. May always appeared in the standard accepted attire—blue uniform, blue cape, and white collar and cap. The children were expected to be well-disciplined and to behave properly. The nurse-governess was to see that they did so.

Children were taught to address their mothers as "Mother, dear"; their fathers as "Sir." May was called "Nurse" or "Nurse May." "Please," "thank you," "yes, m'um" and "no, sir" were all obligatory.

May had a natural gift when it came to working with children. She soon earned the respect and admiration of her employers.

She seemed to sense quickly the emotional needs of her children. Once she was called into a home where the three-year-old was a hopelessly undisciplined tyrant. Nobody knew what to do with young Jenny. A new baby girl had arrived in the family, and May saw at once that the child resented her younger sibling.

"Hello, Jenny," May said as she took the child on her lap. "What a pretty girl you are. And how old might you be?"

"I'm three years old," Jenny said as she held up three fingers.

"My goodness." May looked amazed. "Then maybe you can help with the baby. I'll need lots of help if I'm to look after both of you."

Jenny looked interested. "May I help feed it and bathe it?"

"Of course you may," May said. "You're a big girl now. I'm to teach you to do many things for yourself."

Wherever she went, May stressed the importance of helping and learning, so that the children might feel an important part of the family. She also tried to teach them to think for themselves and to develop their natural curiosity.

At bedtime she told Bible stories and talked about God and Jesus Christ. And May taught this song:

> *Jesus bids me shine, with a clear, pure light,*
> *Like a little candle, burning in the night.*
> *Jesus says He loves me. Jesus says He'll come.*
> *You in your small corner, and I in mine.*

May became impatient with employers who paid too little attention to their children. "Children need parents who do more than poke their heads in the nursery a couple of times a day!" she was known to say indignantly.

One evening after dinner May took her current charge, Wendy, to the drawing room to recite a short poem for her father. The gentleman was reading a newspaper and acted as if he couldn't be bothered. May exploded. "You're the father of this child," she scolded, fists on hips. "You must play a part in your child's life. If she accomplishes something, who's going to tell her 'well done'? Listen to her! Encourage her so she'll wish to learn more!"

Wendy's father harrumped, put down the newspaper, and asked Wendy to recite the poem. "Wendy, that was splendid," he remarked when she was finished. "A fine job. Perhaps Nurse will be good enough to teach you another one for me."

A competent nurse-governess was given a great deal of authority, and May was never shy about using hers.

Once her employer was having a party, and during the evening, a young couple arrived at the nursery. May opened the door and saw at once that they were tipsy.

"We've come to see the baby," the woman announced.

"You are not coming into my nursery," May said.

"But the lady said we could."

May straightened to her full four feet, six inches. "You two have been drinking, and I don't allow anyone who smells of liquor to see this baby. You must come another time!"

"Well! What a nasty little nurse!" the man retorted as the two stomped back down the hall.

Although May was gentle and patient with children, she could be volatile with her employer, particularly if she felt herself to be the victim of an injustice.

One of these eruptions took place during her second assignment. May had the afternoon off and had made plans to meet her mother to attend a concert.

Just as May was leaving, the lady of the house walked into the nursery. "Nurse, take that rug and shake it!" she said, pointing to the floor.

May was furious. "My nursery was swept early this morning and it's been kept nice and clean. There is not a speck on that rug. This is my nursery, and I'm leaving to meet my mother now!"

Her employer repeated the order. "I want you to pick up that rug and clean it!"

Impulsively, May picked up the rug and threw it at the woman. "Now, you step out and shake it! My mother's not to be left standing in the rain!"

May left that home and never went back.

May's responsibilities occasionally included repetitious, time-consuming tasks, and when it came to those, May was ever on the alert for the more efficient way.

Early on, in one of her positions as a maid, the task she hated most was polishing the brass. Houses were filled with brass in those days—doorknobs, fireplace equipment, lamps, stands. Even the gates had brasswork on them. It took a full morning for May to clean the brass.

Exasperated, she went to a shop and asked if there was anything to put on brass so she wouldn't have to polish it every week. The shopkeeper sold her some clear varnish, assuring her she would never have to polish again.

She hurried home, and the first time the lady was out, May varnished every bit of the newly-polished brass, inside and out. From then on, all she had to do was wipe it clean every week. When she told the maids on the street what she had done, they all went out and bought varnish and did the very same thing!

Customarily, May had one afternoon off every week. Most often, she and her mother went to a concert or planned an outing together. After several years of working, May suddenly noticed that for several weeks her mother had seemed preoccupied— like she was thinking of something else.

Not long afterwards Maria said, "May, dear, on your next day off, I must talk with you. Come home, love. We'll have a cup of tea, and I'll tell you what's on my mind."

Chapter 5

Off to America

May's day off arrived, and dutifully she made the familiar trip to her mother's home. After a warm greeting, Maria poured two cups of hot tea and sat down with her daughter.

"May, dear, do you remember James Pollard, the American Yank who used to come to our house so much during the war? You were only a little girl, and he always called you his 'little sweetheart.' He'd come in, look around, and say, 'Where's the little one, the one who's always so full of zip and pep?' "

May replied that she wasn't certain which one James Pollard was. There had been so many Americans coming and going in those days. And that was so long ago.

"Well dear," Mrs. Hansen went on, "he felt so terrible about your accident. He even went to see you once in the hospital. But you wouldn't remember. When he left, he gave me his address and promised that if I ever wanted to send you to America, he'd marry you."

For once May was speechless. "I've written him,

and he's still willing," her mother said. "He's a fine man, May, and he'd make a good home for you. You've suffered enough in England. You deserve to live someplace else."

Leave England, her work, her mother? May had never thought of such a thing. Marry a stranger? Of course, lots of English parents chose husbands and wives for their children. But to leave *forever?*

Deep inside, May knew that her mother was ill. *Possibly she suspects she is dying,* May reasoned. *She wants to make certain I'm cared for.* All kinds of thoughts raced through May's head.

"I'll write to him," she told her mother.

Soon May began getting letters from her Yank. He described the animals, the fields, the garden, how he made his own butter, all about life on his 200-acre farm. He wrote that he had been raised on this farm. His parents, who were both close to ninety, had turned it over to him when they were unable to work any longer. But they continued to live there. May told him that she was a good cook, and although she had never been on a farm, she had a quick mind and could learn anything. A diamond ring arrived, and finally, money for her passage over.

Shortly before she was to leave, May was living with her mother when there was a knock on the door. May answered but didn't recognize the man standing there. He was in terrible shape. "Mama!" she called.

For a moment her mother did not recognize the man either. Then suddenly she embraced him and sobbed, "Oh, my son, my son!"

May had not recognized her second oldest brother, Charlie, nor did he know her. Early in the war, his letters had stopped coming. Mrs. Hansen never heard whether he had been killed or captured. May had ceased talking about Charlie, trying to spare Maria the pain.

As they sat down and recounted the years, Charlie told them he'd been captured in Italy and put in a German concentration camp. He had been badly burned by chlorine gas. "The skin rolled off me," he said slowly and painfully. "It got in ma' throat and it 'erts ta eat 'er talk."

May began to realize the struggle that Charlie faced daily simply to live. He told them that the only way he could eat was to take a teaspoon of kerosene first to numb his throat. When Maria started to pour him a cup of hot tea, he stopped her. "No, Mama, I c'nt drink anything 'ot. It burns ma' throat. I'll 'ave to drink ale." His eyes, too, were affected. He slowly was losing his sight.

"Look at me, Mother," he said with tears in his eyes. "Home to stay. But nothin' to look at. No good at all."

Charlie's homecoming made May even sadder about leaving for America. "I won't last long," he told her, and he urged her to go. "There's nothing left for you here, May. Just a broken-down house and not much family. We'll all be gone soon."

The day before May was to leave, Mrs. Hansen again wrote to James Pollard. "I know you'll make a good husband for my daughter, and she'll not disappoint you," she said. "But I want you to know how much I'll miss her. When May goes, so will the last little bit of sunshine out of my house. She has always been a darling to us all."

At last the bags were packed. May and her mother took the train to Liverpool, where she was to board her ship. That day was the first time that May had ever been out of Monkwearmouth. The city, the people, the hustle and bustle all were strange to her.

In all the confusion of getting on ship, the gangplank went up before May could say good-bye to her mother. The captain was already giving orders to move out. Glancing anxiously at the dock, May ran to the bridge.

"Oh, please, Captain," she begged. "I didn't say good-bye to my mama."

"Lower the gangplanks," the captain called out. "This little one hasn't said good-bye to her mother!"

The sailors lowered the gangplank. May ran halfway down, her mother ran halfway up, and they hugged and kissed one another. "Good-bye, dear. This is the last time we will ever meet," Maria said in a whisper.

May did not want to let go of her mother. Finally the captain himself took her gently by the hand. "Come, dear," he said. "It's time for us to leave." But he waited patiently while May stood on the gangplank and waved until her mother was back on the pier.

The trip to America lasted two weeks. May wasn't long, of course, in getting acquainted with the other passengers. Soon they were laughing, singing, dancing, and telling each other stories.

If loneliness threatened to take over at times, May thought of the verse her mother had taught her when she was a little girl.

> *When you're alone and have no one to love you,*
> *When you're alone and have no one to care,*

You'll never find one half so kind,
Or so willing your troubles to share—Jesus.

One lady on board said to May, "You are too sweet, child, to ever go on a farm. Just wait! You'll be out looking for a job as a nurse-governess before you know it."

Although many of the other passengers were miserable with seasickness, May never suffered a moment. Her father had given her his secret remedy once when she was small—*dog biscuits!* She took along enough to last all the way to America, and she never did get sick.

As the long journey was coming to an end, May's thoughts turned more and more to her future, and her new husband. The ship was to land on the east coast of Canada, in Ottawa. The visas and immigration papers for May could take weeks—even months—to fill out. She could not enter America until all the papers had been processed. When would he come for her?

What would James look like? *He sent me a picture, to be sure,* she thought, *but what can you tell from a picture?* Would he like her? Her scars were hardly noticeable now, and everybody admired her long, golden hair. People even told her she was beautiful.

When would they be married? And what would the farm look like? May had never been on a farm before. Bulls, pigs, roosters, ducks—she had never seen most of the animals Jim wrote of. But they would like her. She had never been afraid of anything.

A government official was waiting for her the day the ship finally landed. He took her to the home of a family named Stewart, where she was to live until the paperwork could be settled. She had her own room and was to help out until James came for her.

On the way to the Stewarts' the official said to May, "Miss Hansen, are you aware that your future husband suffers from shell shock? Sometimes people with that condition can be very irritable. They can even be dangerous."

"I don't know what shell shock is, but I want to marry James," May answered. "He was always very good to my mother."

He went on to explain that when a person has shell shock, he constantly relives the terrible events of the war. Victims may be very sad and cry, or be depressed, or have trouble concentrating. Often they have recurrent nightmares, and the condition seems to stay with them all their lives.

"I can cope with anything," May said matter-of-factly. "After all, I'm a war baby, too. I've seen horrible things all my life. I'll understand what he's going through."

They finally reached their destination, a small town near Ottawa, and Emma Stewart came running out to greet May. They carried in her bags, and soon May was settled with the Stewarts. A month passed before she had a message from James.

May was dusting the floor in her bedroom when Emma came running up the stairs and burst through the door. She handed May a letter. "May, it's from Jim! Hurry! Open it! He must be coming!"

May's hands trembled as she ripped open the letter:

> May, dear,
>   I'll be there on Friday, October 23. We'll be married on Saturday. I'll only have a few days before I have to

be back. I can't leave the farm for long. I'll have to return alone. Your papers are still not in order.

Love, Jim

May was happy, then disappointed—all at once. But she had little time to think about her feelings, there was so much to do. They cleaned the house, started the baking, washed and dried and ironed May's clothes. Her wedding dress had been hanging in the closet for a month, and May had to freshen it up, too.

The day for Jim's arrival drew closer and closer. May wondered what she would say to him. She was not really nervous. Long ago, she had learned to accept whatever happened. She was not afraid; simply curious. And very, very excited.

Friday came. May awoke early, full of anticipation. She could not concentrate on anything; instead she was forever looking out the window.

"Why don't you go sit on the front steps?" laughed Emma.

"Oh, I couldn't do that!" May laughed. "He might think I'm crazy!"

Finally they heard Jim's car, a Model T, coming to a stop in front of the house. May sneaked a look out the window. "Oh, he's so big," she said. "And little me! We'll make quite a couple."

When they opened the door, Jim walked straight over to May and said, "Well, here I am, May. I hope you're not disappointed." He leaned over and gently kissed her.

Mother was right, May thought to herself. *He is a nice man. And really, quite handsome.*

On Saturday, October 24, 1920, Emma and Robert Stewart and another couple who were friends of the

Stewarts went to the church with May and Jim. When the priest pronounced them man and wife, Jim promptly turned around and kissed the wrong woman—the lady friend of Emma's. "Oh, my goodness! She's over there!" she said as she pointed toward May. At the same time Emma was calling out, "That's not her! She's over here by me!" May laughed at all the confusion. "He must have forgotten how small I was," she said gleefully. "He couldn't even find me!"

Since Jim had to return to the farm in a few days, the newlyweds were unable to have a honeymoon. Instead they remained at the Stewart home, taking drives through the lovely Canadian countryside where so many of the trees were still in their glorious fall colors.

"This is so beautiful and quiet," May said over and over again. Most of all, she loved the clean, fresh smells around her. "For the first time, I can't smell the gas and the awful smells of war—houses burning and smoldering all around."

All too soon Jim had to leave. "I'll send for you," he promised, "as soon as I have the papers."

A month passed. Then two. A third had begun when the letter came.

> May, dear,
>   Everything taken care of. Your papers are enclosed. Take a train to Port Huron on January 2. A government official will meet you and put you on a train to Chicago. I will be there to meet you.
>
>   Love, Jim

He was waiting in the station when the train rumbled into Chicago a week later. America! She was really in America! And with her husband!

All the confusion was finally over. May would have a home of her own at last. The ride back to the farm was long, and the sun dipped out of sight before they arrived on the second day of travelling. May breathed in deeply the cold, fresh air. It felt good to be alive!

As they drove onto the property, May heard all kinds of noises: banging, ringing, clanging. "What is that?" she asked her husband. "Where is it coming from?"

"That's a shivaree," Jim laughed. "A shivaree is when you get married and all your friends serenade you."

Sure enough, the yard was full of Jim's neighbors, all wanting to meet the new bride. They had brought food and gifts to welcome May to America.

May soon found life on a farm in northern Wisconsin had little in common with life in Monkwearmouth, England. But she loved America at once and said it took away all the misery and torture she'd been through in England. She loved the friendliness of the people. "Everyone smiles here," she said to Jim one day, "whether they know you or not. One lady told me she loved my accent so much she'd like to sit and listen to me all day!"

She also loved the children. "Such beautiful, handsome children you have in America!" she said so often. Inside, she wept for those crippled, orphaned English youngsters who had suffered so much during the war.

She never did learn to like lettuce. "We never had salads in England," she said, "and I can't eat that kind of food. I'll leave mine for the rabbits!"

Almost every day May discovered something she had never seen before. One day it was the warrior ant. She was out in the fields with her husband when she spotted a large, black ant moving slowly across the ground. She got down on her knees to watch it more closely and saw that it was dragging a worm six or eight inches long. Pretty soon the ant nipped off a piece of the worm, made a little hole, and buried it. Then it went a little further, nipped off another piece, and buried that one. May followed along on her hands and knees until the ant had buried the last of the worm.

"May, what are you doing?" Jim called.

"I know you're going to think me odd, but I'm watching a little ant storing up food for the winter," she shouted back. "Isn't it fascinating?"

May met another unfamiliar creature in the middle of the night, the time a bat flew into her hair. She put her hand to her head and screamed, "Jim, there's something in my hair!"

"That's a bat! Hold still! I'll kill it!" her husband yelled, instantly awake.

"Oh, don't kill it," May wailed. "It didn't mean anything. It was just so scared that it wanted to sit in my hair!"

Jim went after the bat anyway, with May screaming, "Oh, please, let it go!" But this time May didn't have her way.

Even without the bat May managed to find plenty of pets. Any creature that needed a little special attention came under May's doting care: a crippled rooster, an orphaned duck, a pig that was the runt of the litter.

She bottle-fed the tiny piglet from the moment it was born and for the first few months kept it in a box in the kitchen. At about two each morning it ran under the bed and squealed. Jim said, "May, your baby's under the bed. I think she's hungry!" And May always got up to feed her pig.

She later taught the animal to lie on its back and hold the bottle with its legs. Next, it was taught to sit up and roll over. And May gave it a bath every day.

When the pig weighed as much as Jim, he decided they had to do something. He finally gave it to a friend. He didn't have the heart to butcher it himself.

One of May's most memorable achievements was when she helped bring a calf into the world. Her husband showed her how to kneel behind the cow and ease the calf out. But as usual, May did it her way.

She lay down on the barn floor, covered herself with a sack, and braced both feet against the cow. When she saw the head and two feet coming out, she gently pulled, like her husband had told her to do. But alas, it came out suddenly—and landed with a thud right on top of May, feet sprawling in every direction. Jim had to lead the startled calf to its mother while May recovered from her first experience as a veterinarian.

Another time May proved her mettle when Peggy, their black horse, was gored by one of the bulls. "It's a terrible rip," Jim said. "I'm afraid I'm going to have to destroy it."

"You're not going to touch that horse," May warned. "I'll take care of her."

She found some iodine, boric acid, vaseline, string, and a darning needle, and set to work. She used the boric acid, mixed with water, and iodine to clean and sterilize the wound. Then she took the inner skin, sewed it with heavy string, and rubbed vaseline on it. Next she brought the heavy coat together, cleaned it out, and sewed it shut.

All the time she was working, she kept talking. "You better behave yourself, Peggy. I've got to make you well, you know. You had an awful slash!"

Jim watched incredulously and said the stitching would never hold.

"It'll hold," May said. "You just watch and see!"

Peggy was put out to pasture by herself, and May was right. The stitches held. In fact, Peggy delivered her first foal the following year, a healthy colt they named Pollyanna.

May's life on the farm was never lonely, even though they were too isolated to go to town, attend church, or visit friends. Along with the animals, the Pollards soon had children running around the farm—three in eighteen months. First there was a girl, Mary, who was followed by twin boys, Douglas and James. Later they had another girl, Patricia, and one more boy, Charles.

Jim's parents lived to see the first three children, but they died just a few weeks apart, soon after the twins were born.

Jim's father was from England, his mother from Ireland. "Just think," he said again and again, "a tiny little girl came all the way from England where I was born, and she brought me a pair of grandsons. I didn't have any grandchildren so it took a little four-foot lady to have twins for me." He'd hold both boys in his arms and say, "May, which one looks like me?"

May always looked them over very carefully and

then she said, "This one looks like my husband and that one looks like you, Grandpa."

May learned to live with death those first few years of her married life. After Jim's parents died, she received word that her brother, Charlie, was also gone. Soon after that word came that her other brother had died.

She sat down at the table, tears streaming down her cheeks. Little Jimmy came to her. "Mama, you're crying, aren't you?"

By then Douglas and Mary had joined their brother. "Yes, children, there's been another death in my family—this time, my last brother. You know, it's not very good when they go one by one like that. Only my mother and one sister are left."

Mary reached up and wiped the tears off her mother's face. "Don't cry, Mama. Everything will be all right." A few months later there came an airmail letter from May's sister in England. "Mother has died," it said. "We are the only ones left."

But May had to get on with her life. After all, she had five young children, a husband, and plenty of work on the farm to keep her busy.

As the children grew older, May told them how she had baptized them as babies. Each time, she had filled a bowl with warm water, holding the new infant in her arms, and had made the sign of the Cross on the little forehead with water. Then she had sprinkled the child and had said solemnly, "I baptize you in the name of the Father, the Son, and the Holy Ghost."

Although they rarely could go to church, May taught her children about Jesus Christ. Someday, she said, they would find their own churches and worship the Lord in a congregation. Her Christianity went beyond Sundays-only. One of her boys was having trouble with schoolwork one day, and he came to his mother, very discouraged. "I can't do it. I just can't do it," he said.

"Why don't you go to your room and talk with God about what you can't do?" May asked.

He went to his room and was back in a half hour. "I did it!" he said. "I asked God, and I did it!"

"You see," May said, "you can't live without Him. He's there to help you whenever you need Him."

May was a natural storyteller. At night, she gathered the children around her feet and told them stories: fairy tales, adventures, mysteries, and stories about Jesus. The children hung on every word, for May always left them wondering what would happen in the next episode.

At Christmas and Easter she read from the Bible, and the children asked questions about Jesus. "Isn't it awful how Jesus suffered so much for us and for our sins?" Douglas asked one night. "And He never did anything wrong."

May also had a beautiful voice, and the children often heard her playing the piano and singing hymns, including her favorite, "The Old Rugged Cross," long after they had gone to bed.

Sometimes, Jim came in the house to find his wife scurrying under tables and chairs, playing tag and hide-and-seek with the children. "There are some advantages to being small," he told her, laughing. "You can hide in the tiniest places, and nobody will ever find you!"

Along with the stories and games, May was a strict disciplinarian. She insisted on good manners and respect for authority. She was also a hard worker and expected as much from her children.

Besides the personal talks with God that were at the hub of her daily life, May lived according to strict biblical dictates, which she passed on to her children.

She was very fussy, for example, about honesty and the importance of never taking anything that did not belong to them. She had no tolerance for any kind of prejudice and warned her children never to judge people by their color, clothes, or education. "There is only one place God judges a person," she said, "and that is where the heart is."

"Always be your own person," she said over and over again. "Don't try to imitate someone else. You were given your own personality and your own talents, so use them. Be natural. Be yourself."

May's children were as fearless and loving toward animals as their mother was. On their way home from school one day, Mary and Pat saw a family of baby skunks, which they mistook for kittens. The two girls sat in the field playing with them for a while, then hurried home.

When they burst through the kitchen door they were talking at once. "Oh, Mama, we saw the most beautiful black kittens on the way home. They had beautiful white stripes. . . ."

"What you saw are skunks and you smell terrible!" May interrupted. "Take off all your clothes. I'll have to bury everything!"

As the years passed, Jim had more and more bouts with shell shock. Sometimes May saw him standing in the field trembling and crying. Those times she would call one of the children to help bring him back into the house. "Come on, love," she said tenderly, "come into the house. You must be cold out there." She took him in and held him close, cuddling him like a baby.

She explained to the children that their father was ill and might always have that sickness. "Oh, it must have been awful for him in the war," she said, wiping away a tear. Sometimes Jim went to the hospital for two or three weeks, but May never went to visit. The hospital was too far away, and her husband insisted it was better for her to care for the farm and the children.

The children were well taught and were able to do many chores on the farm. Douglas was milking a cow when he was five years old. "Why, just look at all the farmers I have running around," May often said, laughing.

Between Jim's hospital visits, the Pollards enjoyed long periods of tranquility when it seemed that nothing could disturb the contentment of their lives.

On one of these lovely days, a glorious summer afternoon, Jim was harvesting the summer wheat, and May was tending the children. Then disaster struck.

Several nearby farmers came running through the fields shouting, "Fire! Forest fire! It's headed this way! Houses are burning down! We need every man we can get!"

"We'll put your wife and kids down the well!" one of them shouted to Jim. "They'll be safe there! Get some boards! Mrs. Pollard, get some blankets and milk for the babies. Hurry!"

The men lowered several wide boards down the thirty-foot well, and by then May was back with a basket for the twins, plenty of blankets, and milk. They told May not to worry. If the fire did come, it would pass over the well. She and the children would be safe.

The night was long for May. The children were restless and making them comfortable wasn't easy in those close, damp quarters. But she sang to them, told them stories, and reassured them that Daddy would come soon.

By morning May could smell smoke, and she knew that the fire was raging toward them. She heard the roar of flames as the fire reached the farm and the crackling of timber as buildings came crashing down. May wept as she thought about her husband, his failing health, and the heartache of having to start all over again. What would the farm look like when they lifted her out of the well? Would anything be left?

She soon found out. The men returned, and May was lifted up into a strange black world of charred earth, heaps of smoldering ashes, and grotesque, smoky shapes where the buildings had stood only a few hours earlier. Everything was gone: animals, furniture, clothing, letters from Jim, pictures of the children, every evidence of their life together. Nothing was left.

The Pollards moved in with a distant neighbor until a second house was built. But Jim was never the same. His war injuries were returning to plague him, and less than a year after they moved into their new home, Jim began a long hospitalization. May and the children ran the farm as best they could.

A second tragedy occurred when the children were

older. Although the twins were only ten, they were
doing men's work. The girls were cooking, baking,
canning, and looking after May's chickens. Jim was
still hospitalized. The family faced obstacles and
adversity every day, but they were managing to keep
their lives together. Each day the world looked a little
brighter.

A devastating tornado knocked them to the ground
again. When the storm had gone, once more the
house was gone. There was no one to turn to. The
Pollards had no car, no telephone, no close neighbors. The season was late fall, and the weather was
cold. There was no food.

The only building left standing was the small
chicken shack on one side of the farm. May took the
children there. There were holes in the walls, so they
had little protection from the wind. May began
wishing she could at least start a fire. Her hands were
blue from cold.

She fell on her knees in the tiny shack and prayed,
"Oh, Jesus. I need help and I need it badly. You gave
me these beautiful children. Please save us now from
destruction." She felt better after praying, like a
heavy burden had been lifted from her shoulders.
She could almost sense Someone in the room saying,
Have no fear, May. You're going to be all right.

Minutes later there was a knock on the door. The
visitor was a young boy, and he said, "We thought
you might have been hit. Don't worry. I'll get some
help for you."

A group of men soon arrived, and one of them took
May and the children to stay with a neighboring family. Then they began to rebuild the shack for the Pol-

lards. They put in new walls, new flooring, and installed a ceiling, making it livable. Next they put in a stove, chopped wood, and stacked a supply of logs around the building. They collected beds, a table, chairs, blankets, clothing, dishes, food—all the necessities. In less than two weeks the little house was ready for the Pollards to move in.

May was ecstatic. "Oh, thank You, Jesus," she prayed. "You have performed a miracle for us. You brought us all these things from people we don't even know. And they came as soon as I asked for Your help. This is truly a miracle!"

Jim returned to live with his family, but he was never well again. However, he had been a good father while he was able. He had taught his boys well, and they could work almost as hard as he had. May bought more and more chickens and managed to sell enough eggs to buy the groceries.

In 1943 Jim Pollard died. May sold the farm and took the two girls to Milwaukee to finish their education while she found a job. The boys all joined the armed services.

In Milwaukee she found a minister to care for the girls, and an employment agency found her a position at once as a nurse-governess. "We don't have many authentic nurse-governesses in Milwaukee," she was told. "You'll always have a job."

So May was at work in her trade once again, and she still knew her business. In her first position three-year-old Billy was scheduled to have an operation. He was terrified, so May went along and took his favorite toy car.

On the way to the hospital she told Billy that she

was going to buy some gasoline for his car, and it would smell "real bad." When the doctor was ready to operate, she said, "Well, Billy, it's time to put the gasoline in your car. But before it will go, you have to sniff some of that gasoline. So you take a real good sniff and, boy, will that car make a rumble!"

By that time the ether was turned on and Billy was out. "The story was a kind deed," May told the doctor, "so the boy would go peacefully."

"I've never met a nurse-governess before," the doctor said, laughing, "but you sure know some tricks. I'll have to try that one sometime!"

For the first time in her life May had a chance to travel with the families who employed her. She spent six weeks in New York, six months in Pennsylvania, and many summers in Naples, Florida—all places she had never been before.

"It's nice to see those places," she said, "but I'm working, just like I'd be doing in Milwaukee. When you're a nurse-governess, you stick to your work." She was always glad to get home and be close to her girls again.

May's work as a nurse-governess in England had been cut short when her mother sent her to America. After a few years in Milwaukee her work was interrupted once again—this time by a man named Joe Lemke.

Chapter 6

May, Meet Joe Lemke

Joe Lemke was born in Manitowoc, Wisconsin, a city located about eighty miles north of Milwaukee on Lake Michigan. With thirteen children in the family, every member had to learn to fend for himself early. Joe was fifth in line. He quit high school when his mother died and went out to earn a living.

He chose construction work and began working his way south to Milwaukee, where he knew he could find jobs. Always close with his money, he even managed to save during the Depression. In 1932 he was able to pick up the lien on a one-room shack on Pewaukee Lake, twenty miles west of Milwaukee, and have a place of his own. He had just turned twenty-eight years old.

Although jobs were scarce during the Depression, Joe had a lot of pride, and when his construction boss lowered his hourly wage from sixty-five to forty cents, Joe quit. "If I'm going to starve, I might as well starve at home!" he told his boss.

He didn't work for over a year, but he had some savings. The bank where he kept his money folded, but another bank bought it out and paid fifty cents on the dollar. Joe got half his money back: five hundred dollars. The windfall was like five thousand dollars today. It got Joe by.

Joe's needs and wants were basic, and they never included an automobile. Streetcars, buses, and friends' cars carried him everywhere he wanted to go. "I've never been behind the wheel of a car," he maintained steadfastly, "and I never care to."

When World War II broke out Joe was thirty-seven. He was inducted into the Army in June of 1942 and sent to Africa to work in a station hospital unit. When the war was over he returned to Milwaukee and construction work.

Six years passed, and Joe's life changed little. He worked during the day and came home to his little shack at night. At forty-four he was still a bachelor. "Haven't found the right girl yet" is how he put it.

But at a dance on a lovely summer night in 1948, Joe Lemke found the right girl. She was a pretty little thing, less than five feet tall with golden-blond hair. She was wearing a beautiful red gown with a hoop skirt that she said had come all the way from Switzerland.

Her name was May—May Pollard—and she had come all the way from a place called Monkwearmouth on the northern coast of England. She told Joe that she was a nurse-governess in a home in Milwaukee. "A nurse-governess?" Joe looked puzzled. "What is that supposed to be?"

May laughed and told him about her training in England and her succession of positions in Milwaukee. He was fascinated with this little English lady. He found her clipped British accent as charming as her quick sense of humor.

A few days later Joe proposed. "I'm not perfect, May, but will you marry me?"

"Well," May answered, "I don't care to know all your shortcomings, but you are a bachelor and you're getting older. I'll soon be that way, too." So they agreed to be married.

"Say, on your next day off," Joe said, "I'll show you the place I'd like to buy for us. My little shack suited me fine, but it's no place for a lady. I could sell it and maybe buy this one." Accordingly, the following week Joe took May to see a little cottage that was for sale on Pewaukee Lake. May said it was fine.

Of course the cottage needed work. The wood floors were old and worn. Wallpaper was peeling off the walls. There were neither closets nor kitchen cupboards. The yard was littered with rocks, branches, and other debris. But May and Joe were clever and industrious, and they knew they could fix the place up.

They figured out how much money they would have if they pooled their resources. There was enough to cover the asking price, so they decided to complete the transaction on May's next day off. Afterwards there would still be time to get married.

The ceremony was brief, and May and Joe promptly moved in and went to work. They added paneling, new flooring, a large closet, and kitchen cupboards. They papered, painted, scrubbed, and varnished until their cottage was just the way they wanted it to be.

Next they tackled the yard. Joe began tearing down

an old building that was deteriorating at the back of the property. He hired someone to help him lay a concrete roof on top of the basement and covered it with gravel. "Now I have a place to chop my wood and keep my tools," he told May. "And if we ever need a bomb shelter, we've got it!"

In the meantime May hauled away branches, rocks, and leaves, often on her days off when Joe was at work. She planted trees, bushes, flowers, plants, and vegetables, and she hung bird feeders, filling them to the brim with sunflower seeds.

May had to continue her work in Milwaukee to make ends meet, coming home weekends to be with Joe. Sometimes she found odd jobs for him where she was working, as a gardener or handyman.

They were always busy, always working at something. For four years, life for the Lemkes was routine, predictable, and tranquil. They had much to be thankful for.

Then, in 1952, on one of those lovely Wisconsin summer afternoons, the Lemkes' life changed, drastically and permanently. They had been puttering in their yard, occasionally watching a few fishing boats drifting lazily on the lake. Warm sunlight filtered through the trees, and a soft breeze was moving in quietly from the south.

They were jarred from their tranquility by the sudden appearance of one of their neighbors, a dentist, who lived down the road. People usually kept to themselves on Pewaukee Lake, and the Lemkes knew only a few of their neighbors. They had never met the dentist, so May was a bit uneasy.

"Are you Mrs. Lemke?" the intruder inquired.

"Why, yes," May answered. "Why do you ask?"

"Someone called my house and left a message for you. They said you don't have a phone."

May hurried away with him. Who would be calling her? One of the children? Was someone hurt? She dialed the number. "This is May Lemke," she said. "What did you wish?"

"I'm calling from a hospital in Milwaukee," the voice at the other end of the line said. "We heard that you had married and moved out to Pewaukee. We've been looking for you. You may be the one to help us out."

"What is it?" May asked

"We have a six-month-old baby here who's had his eyes taken out. He also has cerebral palsy and is retarded. He won't live long. We thought maybe with your background and all, you'd take him and look after him. The parents don't want him. There's nobody to take him—no family, no nothing. Would you think about it, Mrs. Lemke?"

"I don't need to think about it," May said. "I'm moved in, and I can take him. I have a little vacation right now, so bring him out."

"But don't you want to discuss it with your husband, Mrs. Lemke? He might need time to think about it," the woman inquired.

"I know my husband," May said flatly. "If I choose to do something, he won't object. He's a good man, and he has a soft spot in him."

May's work as a nurse-governess had earned her a reputation around Milwaukee for being excellent with children. Several of the nurses at the hospital had heard stories of May's expertise with her young charges, but nobody seemed to know who she had married or where she lived. When they finally tracked her down that summer afternoon, she was between jobs.

A nurse brought the baby to the Lemkes the day after the phone call. His name was Leslie. Joe took the tiny infant, wrapped in a blanket and wearing a blue knitted cap, and held him carefully in his arms. Joe had not been around children much since he left home as a teenager, and now he was nearly fifty years old. But there was a tenderness in his eyes as he looked down at the baby, and a sadness on his face as he saw the terrible disabilities of the child.

It took only a glance to see that something was wrong. Born prematurely and weighing only three pounds at birth, Leslie still looked like a newborn infant—long and very thin. The sunken sockets where his eyes had been made his other features seem out of proportion. His hair was reddish-brown, his skin pale and wan. Saddest of all was the way he lay in Joe's arms: like a flimsy doll without movement or response.

May took the baby from Joe, tears streaming down her cheeks. "Oh, Joe, he looks terrible! So forlorn, so long and thin and helpless. But God loves all children, even this little creature. We'll just see what we can do."

They took the baby inside and talked about where to start. "We need a good formula," May said, "one that will begin to put some weight on him. Mama always used slippery elm paste for the sick babies in England. Joe, you stay with Leslie, and I'll take a bus to that health store in Pewaukee. They might have something."

May soon returned, carrying a small parcel. "They had it, Joe. It's a slippery elm powder. I'll just mix a teaspoonful with a pint of milk and water and add a bit of sugar. I want it sweet, but not too sweet." May mixed the formula and held the bottle to Leslie's mouth. "Try a little, love. You'll like this," she said softly. Leslie didn't seem to understand. He lay motionless, his tongue pushing out the nipple. "Suck, baby, you must suck it in," May encouraged. Still, he lay motionless.

May put her mouth against his cheek, making loud sucking sounds. Then she put the bottle in his mouth, hoping he might catch on. She kept up the procedure most of the afternoon, sucking on the baby's cheek and putting the bottle in his mouth, over and over again. At last, he began to suck a little, tentatively at first. As the warm milk trickled down his throat, he grew bolder. Pretty soon he was sucking with the zest of a normal, healthy infant. May danced with him around the room. "Baby," she cried out, "you're going to live!"

Besides the formula, May had to do something about the sockets where Leslie's eyes had been. They were still red, and mucous was seeping through the tissue.

The nurse had told May that Leslie's eyes were cloudy at birth, and as the weeks passed, he had not opened them as normal infants do. Doctors were unable to dilate the pupils, and both corneas continued to be cloudy and scarred. Later there was a discharge from the eyes and they became swollen. There was apparently no sight in either eye.

The nurse was not clear as to what had caused the inflammation of Leslie's eyes. "It's hard to pinpoint these things," she had said. "It could be any number of diseases or circumstances—we don't always know." When Leslie was four months old, the symptoms were worsening, and doctors removed Leslie's left eye. Six weeks later they removed his right eye as well.

May made a boric acid solution and dropped it into the empty sockets several times a day to keep them clean. When the sockets were healed, the eyelids closed by themselves. They always stayed shut after that.

Leslie continued to suck well and swallow his formula when May fed him. He seemed to be thriving on the concoction, but he wasn't doing anything else. He hardly moved at all, and his arms and legs were limp. May often lifted them hopefully, but they always dropped back down again.

He rarely cried or whimpered like babies do when they're hungry. He hardly made a sound. May couldn't tell if he was asleep or awake, because his eyes were always shut. Finally she decided to treat him like a normal baby and feed him every four hours. He always ate, and the food stayed down.

Months passed. May got down on her knees every night, praying for Jesus to "do something with Leslie." But still he remained silent and helpless.

Leslie was about a year old when May started him on solid food. She began with small portions of oatmeal and hard-boiled eggs, mashed up with butter. She didn't give him much, only a bit at a time. At first, Leslie spat the food out. He didn't seem to know what to do with it.

But slowly he began to swallow a little, and it

wasn't long before he seemed to enjoy eating. But progress was slow. Meals were very small until he was several years old.

As soon as Leslie was eating fairly well, May decided to teach him to drink from a cup. The first time she tried, she put a little bit of water in a tiny cup and held it to his mouth. No response. May finally had to pour the water into his mouth and let it drain down his throat. Weeks went by before Leslie made any effort at all to try to drink by himself.

By this time May's daughters, who had remained in close contact with their mother, were getting concerned. After all, May was close to fifty. Although she *seemed* to have an inexhaustible supply of energy . . . well, she couldn't go on forever. They knew that the longer she kept Leslie, the harder it would be for her to give him up. Both girls lived in Wisconsin and wrote their mother frequently. Occasionally they came to visit.

On one of her trips to Pewaukee daughter Pat realized fully how hard her mother was working. "Mother," she said, "what are you doing? Are you giving up your work as a nurse-governess?"

"Yes, I've earned enough money," May answered. "I've got my husband now. I can't go back to work, not with a baby like this. I have a job to do for Jesus now, and I'm going to do it. I could never leave this boy."

When Leslie was still physically inactive at almost three years of age, May decided to take him to a doctor. Maybe he could tell her some way to get Leslie crawling and walking. Even though he had cerebral palsy, May thought that Leslie ought to be making attempts to move around. The doctor shook his head. "I really don't know what to tell you, May," he said. "It's hard to tell how long it will take. But you've got a lot of faith. Maybe something will happen."

"I know that God can do things," May said. "If He can do them for others, then He can do them for me!" *But I do think I've waited long enough,* she thought to herself. She decided to go home and wait a little longer.

May cuddled Leslie in her arms every day, rocking him and singing softly to him. "I want him to know that he's loved," she said over and over again to Joe, "to know he has a mother and a father who love him just like other children."

Despite May's gentleness, Leslie always tensed, startled, as if he were frightened whenever she picked him up. He never relaxed his body against her like a normal baby. He was more like a plastic baby, rigid, with rarely a cry, never a smile.

But May refused to give up. "Children respond to love," she told Joe. "They can feel it in your body when you hold them close. I know he'll feel it eventually. It just takes more time with a child like this."

When the neighborhood children heard that there was a baby at the Lemke home, they began streaming over to play with him. But when they saw that he couldn't respond to them, they soon stopped coming. One of the neighbors brought over a teddy bear for Leslie. "That's kind of you," May said, "but he won't know what it is."

"Give it to him anyway," the woman said. "Maybe someday he'll be able to play with it."

When Leslie was almost five years old, he began to

relax a little and lay his head against May's body when she rocked him. But he never lifted a hand to touch her.

Undaunted, May tried to think of some way to get more movement in Leslie's arms and legs. A ritual emerged. She laid him on his bed and massaged his legs, arms, and back with sweet oil—twice a day, morning and evening. Then she exercised his legs, moving them up and down against his body. Finally she went through a routine with his arms.

Yet even this therapy did not seem to help. When May tried to sit Leslie up, his body still collapsed. His bones seemed to be made of spaghetti.

Joe brought home an infant chair for Leslie. The child was six years old, thin and frail. "Maybe we can sit him outside to get some sun and fresh air," he said to May. Leslie slumped forward in the chair, so they had to tie him securely with a cord.

In the summers May laid him naked on a soft rug in the sunshine almost every day. She hoped that the warmth and lack of restraint might encourage him to move around a little. But he never did. He was a distressing sight, a long, thin, pitiful little creature.

When May worked around the house, she always made sure that Leslie was close to her, so he could hear her and know that she was around. She propped him up with pillows on the sofa or laid him flat on his bed. Winters, when Joe made a fire in the fireplace, he laid Leslie on the rug in front of it where he'd be warm.

May chattered to the boy constantly. If she wasn't talking, she was singing.

"I'm making an apple pie for you today, love."

"That's a fire that you smell. But you can't touch it. It is hot and it burns."

"That's Daddy coming home, love. Can you hear him? He's going to pick you up and cuddle you."

Still no response, never a sound. May never knew if Leslie was hurt or needed anything. She had to do everything for him.

Again and again concerned friends and neighbors told May to put Leslie in an institution. "He'll never do anything or learn anything. Look what you're doing to yourselves," they said. "You and Joe are giving up your whole lives for that boy."

Leslie's doctor began to suggest that the time was coming when institutional care would be necessary. He applauded May's patience and devotion but warned her that when Leslie was older, she might not be able to keep up the responsibility. After all, she was in her mid-fifties, and Leslie was a seven-year-old boy.

But May wouldn't listen. She only prayed more. "Oh, Jesus, help me reach this little boy. Please, show me what to do. Help me to turn this little creature into a more normal human being."

She cried enough for both of them. She held Leslie so close that her tears ran down his cheeks as well as her own. Sometimes she put his little hands on her face so he could feel her tears.

Every facet of May's life continued to involve Leslie. If she needed to go shopping, Leslie went along, even though she had to carry him. Although he was still a thin, frail child, it was becoming harder for May—so tiny herself—to lift and carry him.

Since the Lemkes didn't own a car, May always

called a cab to take her to the grocery store. Once inside the store she handed her list to a checkout girl or simply told her what she needed. The girl then shopped for May, bagged her groceries, called another cab, and carried the groceries out. If May had to make another stop in her shopping expedition, she went through the routine all over again.

May and Leslie were well-known all over Pewaukee. Policemen were constantly on the alert for the tiny little Englishwoman carrying the retarded boy. When she crossed the street, they were there beside her, fearful that her pint-sized frame might give out or not be seen by motorists.

As going places with Leslie became more and more difficult, May decided it was time to teach him how to walk. Although he was small for a seven-year-old, he weighed nearly fifty pounds, and she knew the boy could not be carried around forever. She certainly didn't want Leslie spending the rest of his life lying around doing nothing.

May had an idea. She took a three-inch-wide leather belt and strapped Leslie to herself around the waist, with Leslie standing directly behind her. Since Leslie couldn't hold on by himself, Joe made a little leather loop for his hands on each side of the belt. This way May could grasp Leslie's hands and walk, dragging him along behind.

May called the operation "trailing." The idea was to let Leslie feel how she walked in the hope that he would imitate her. May walked with him almost every day for three years, until he was nearly ten years old, but Leslie never took a single step.

Neighbors often saw the tiny Mrs. Lemke walking

slowly up and down the road, young Leslie trailing behind. "Some of the neighbors think you're being cruel, May, but most of us understand that you're trying to help him," encouraged Agnes Myers, a longtime friend.

One summer afternoon when Leslie was nearly nine years old, May was sitting by the lake, looking out at the water and wondering what to do next. The trailing wasn't producing any noticeable results. What else could she try?

As she stared at the water, a new idea came to her. *The lake! Why not the lake?* she thought. *Water ought to be good for a child like Leslie. Joe is a good swimmer. He can take him in!*

As soon as Joe came home from work that night, May laid out her plan. "You can swim, Joe. Take Leslie in the water, swim around with him, and bump him up and down. Then maybe he'll start to move."

After dinner Joe carefully eased Leslie into the cool water. He swam with him, bounced him up and down, played with him—but nothing happened. Finally Joe lay on his back in the water, letting the little boy rest on him. Patches of orange sunlight left traces in the sky where the sun had retreated a few minutes before. The water was still except for a few muffled ripples from flying fish. Joe silently wondered if Leslie felt as peaceful as Joe did. Neither his body nor his face showed any signs of content—or discontent. There was no way to know how Leslie felt.

From then on Joe took Leslie into the lake regularly, at night after work and on weekends. He splashed him around, held him to his chest while he swam on his back, and bounced him up and down. He talked to him often, trying to make him laugh, hoping to stir some emotion, some response. They usually stayed in the water so long that May said Leslie looked like a withered old carcass when Joe brought him ashore.

Late one Sunday afternoon in the middle of summer, Joe was floating lazily on his back, holding the boy. Joe was close to sixty now, and he was weary after the sessions in the water. He closed his eyes, drifting a little in the gently rolling waves.

A scream from May brought him abruptly to his feet. "What's wrong? What happened?" he called out.

"Did you see it? Did you see it, Joe?"

"Did I see what?" he shouted.

"Leslie! He moved his hands! He did it himself! I saw it, Joe! Thank God! Thank God! Leslie's moving!"

Chapter 7
The Miracle

That first sign of activity in Leslie wasn't much—only a tiny, almost imperceptible movement of the hand.

But May hadn't missed it. She had been with Leslie too long not to notice a change, no matter how small.

Freshly inspired, May and Joe tried a new routine. It started with Joe taking Leslie down to the lake and exercising him in the lapping water, moving him back and forth. Joe tenderly glided the frail, limp boy through the water for at least thirty minutes, sometimes an hour. At the end of the session he carried Leslie, dripping and wrinkled, up on the shore.

Then May took over. She toweled him off, chattering and singing as she briskly rubbed him dry. After dressing him she carried him to a wire fence that bordered the lot. She wrapped Leslie's elastic fingers around the netting, hoping he'd try to hang on by himself and hold his body erect. Time after time, May stood him up, attached his hands, and then watched disappointedly as Leslie's body buckled and dropped to the ground.

May kept up the trailing, too, every day, around and around the yard, up and down, back and forth, hoping and praying for some sign of movement, some indication that her untiring efforts were getting through to him.

Neighbors watched the diminutive Mrs. Lemke carrying and trailing the sixty-pound boy who was almost as tall as she was, and they were appalled. "Why don't you put him someplace?" one of them asked. "It's been nearly ten years, and he's still not doing much of anything. May, you're wasting your life away."

"I'm not wasting my life," May retorted. "I'm doing something for an innocent boy who will be something someday. You wait and see. I believe in God, and He's going to do it!"

Even her daughter, Mary, approached her gently. "You might have to give him up, Mother. It's going to break your heart, I know."

But May persisted and, if anything, became more stubborn and determined. "I'm not going to give him up for you or for anybody else. It might take me all my life, but I'm going to do something with this boy. If God says He can do things, then He can do them for me. If He doesn't, then I'm just going to pester Him to death!"

So May went back to work: trailing, lifting, carrying, in the water, out of the water, standing, holding, massaging—everything she could think of. Leslie still could not hold on to the fence.

Feeling a little discouraged, May walked down to

the lake one afternoon. She sat at the edge of the
water, near the spot where Joe was playing with Leslie and watched them impassively, half-concentrating
on what steps to take next. Nothing she was doing
seemed to work.

Suddenly her eyes raced to Leslie. *Am I dreaming?*
she thought. *Or is someone playing tricks on me?* But she
wasn't dreaming. She could see it. It was true!
"Joe!!!" He could have heard her halfway across the
lake.

"Joe! He's moving! His legs are moving! His arms
are moving! His whole body is moving! He's
splashing! Joe, it worked! It worked! That boy is
going to walk!"

Excitedly they took Leslie out of the water. May's
hands trembled as she wrapped him in a towel. She
was laughing and crying all at once. "Help me, Joe.
Help me get him dressed. I can't do anything right.
Joe, do you think he can stand now?" Joe pulled Leslie's shirt over his head and slipped on his shoes.
They both helped him to the fence.

Joe stood Leslie up, then fastened his fingers
securely on the netting of the fence. May began as
she had a hundred times before. "Come on, love. Try
to hang on, just for a few seconds. Hold on tight.
Come on, baby, you can do it! You can . . ." May
caught her breath. "Joe! Joe! He did it! He stood
alone! Leslie stood alone!"

Leslie wavered in the air for only a few seconds,
and then he fell in a heap, but May was ecstatic. "See,
God is listening," she said. "He does things for other
people, and He does them for me, too. I just have to
keep after Him!"

An early venture into Pewaukee Lake for Joe and Leslie.

May on her wedding day. She was barely 18 when she married James Pollard.

Leslie, almost 10,
stands alone.

The morning of "The Miracle." Soon after, Leslie's frail body began to fill out.

An early practice session with May and Joe.

Leslie's first concert. As ever, May is an irrepressible emcee.

Joe and May at a recent concert, waltzing while Leslie performs.

Leslie plays a favorite — "I Was Nobody's Baby But I'm Somebody's Baby Now."

The Lemkes at home. May coaches Leslie with praise and humor.

The Milwaukee Journal by Dale Guldan

May's boy —
an incredible
story of love.

As before, May brought Leslie to the fence daily to stand. The seconds began stretching into minutes, and after several weeks, Leslie could stand for several minutes, holding onto the fence. Then May or Joe carried him into the house, exhausted.

They kept the ritual up for months. Still Leslie did not walk. May refused to be discouraged. "I can wait forever," she said. "At least he's standing by himself."

One cool fall evening Joe made a crackling fire in the fireplace and propped Leslie up on several large pillows on the sofa. May was sitting with him, staring at the fire and trying to think of some way to get Leslie to walk.

"Maybe if I took him to a clinic of some kind . . ." she mused to Joe aloud. "Don't they have places where they teach children to walk?" Joe nodded that he was sure they did.

She called her doctor the next day, and he told her of a clinic in Milwaukee where they specialized in physical therapy. "Perhaps they can help Leslie," he said encouragingly.

She got up the next morning and called her neighbor Agnes to see if she would drive her to Milwaukee. Otherwise she would have to take the bus, most likely changing several times, and Leslie was getting too heavy for that. A cab to Milwaukee would be far too expensive. Agnes often drove May places and never took money (so May always bought her something over her protestations).

"Of course I'll take you," Agnes said, without a moment's hesitation. "When do you want me to come?" May wondered sometimes what she would do without Agnes Meyer, her closest friend on the lake. Agnes lived in the second cottage south of the Lemkes and had been there almost as long as May and Joe—nearly sixteen years. Agnes was as soft-spoken as May was effervescent. The two had formed a strong bond over the years. Agnes could always be depended on.

May washed and dressed Leslie, dressed herself, and by 9:30, Agnes was already at the door. Agnes drove the twenty miles to Milwaukee, and after asking for directions several times, finally found the clinic.

Agnes helped carry Leslie inside. After a half-hour wait a therapist called them in. He tried a few tests with Leslie to see if the boy would respond. He lifted his arms and legs and massaged his body, then began asking May questions.

"How long has he been this way?"

"What have you tried with him?"

"What changes have you seen?"

"I'm sorry, Mrs. Lemke," he finally said, almost apologetically, "but I don't think we can do anything for this boy. I don't know what to tell you. Working with him will take a long time and a lot of effort, and you still might not get him walking. You can keep doing what you're doing and maybe someday you'll get him moving around. But I can't promise anything."

"I *will* get him walking someday," May said as she carried her helpless son toward the door. "I surely *will* get him walking!"

May returned to the old routine: trailing, water exercise, propping Leslie by the fence—hour after hour and day after day. As they turned the corner of winter and Leslie passed his tenth birthday, she began to notice a change in him.

At first it was hard to put her finger on. Did he seem to cock his head—just a bit—when she was talking? Did his body tighten—just a speck—when she was near? The change was miniscule, but she was sure he was beginning to *listen.*

She noticed the difference again when he was standing by the fence a few days later. He seemed as if he was paying attention to her. His body, instead of being limp and sluggish, was poised and alert.

She moved close to him and held out her arms. "Come to me, love, turn around." Leslie *moved!* She called out again. "Come to me, love! You're a boy already! Walk to Mama! Over here!" Leslie moved his foot slightly.

May called out again. "Come to me, love! Walk to me!" He fell in her arms. May was jubilant. Leslie had taken his first step. He would walk someday! It would only take time.

With renewed vigor May took Leslie out several times a day and watched him move his feet, little by little, inch by inch, until he could slowly move his body along the fence. The pace was very, very slow at first, but *he was walking.*

Sometimes May watched him from a window, moving so haltingly, agonizing over every step. And she wept all the tears that had been filling up in her. She cried because he still could not get out of bed, could not hold anything to his mouth properly, could not drink by himself, could not do much of anything by himself.

When Leslie was twelve years old, May began to pray a new prayer for her son. She prayed that he might have a gift, something to give his life meaning. Several times a day, she implored, "Dear Lord, the Bible says that you gave each of us a talent. Please help me find the talent in this poor boy who lies there most of the day and does nothing."

Soon after May began praying this way for Leslie, asking for a talent, she noticed another difference in him. Whenever he felt a taut piece of string or cord, he plucked it with his fingers. He seemed to respond to the activity and draw satisfaction from it. May was puzzled by this strange, new behavior. She watched him day after day, searching for some meaning. Could Leslie be making music? Was he trying to strum to some mysterious tempo?

What else could they do? Leslie's birthday was coming up in January. He would be thirteen years old. Why not buy him a piano? The idea seemed silly, to be sure, but May could play a little by ear. She could play some simple tunes and show him how the keys make different sounds. If he liked to strum a chord, why wouldn't he enjoy hitting the keys of a piano? At least a piano could produce sounds. A piece of string could not do that.

She and Joe began searching through the newspaper ads for a used piano. They couldn't afford much, but surely they could find something within their budget. "I found one!" Joe said one evening as he was scanning the columns. "It's two hundred fifty dollars. What do you think, May?"

"Let's call them," May said. "If it sounds good, we'll go and look at it." It sounded fine, so Joe and

May got Leslie ready, called a cab, and went to see the piano. They talked it over. "Can you deliver?" Joe asked.

The man said he had a trailer, and if Joe and May would take it, he would deliver it the following day.

"Do you think we did the right thing?" May asked on the way home.

"What's the difference?" Joe answered. "You like to play the piano. If Leslie isn't interested, you can enjoy it yourself."

When the man came with the piano the next day, May asked him to put it in Leslie's bedroom, close to his bed. "Are you sure you want it there, ma'am?" he asked in disbelief. "That's an awfully small room. Wouldn't you rather have it in the living room or on that porch?"

"No, it's his piano." May had made up her mind. "Someday the boy might play it, you know."

He looked at her incredulously. "Well, if that's where you want it. . . ." He and his husky young son moved the piano into Leslie's bedroom. They could hardly get it through the narrow door, and there was barely space left to move around. "Thanks a lot, lady," he said as he left. "I hope he likes his piano."

May began to play simple little tunes for Leslie. Then she ran his hands over the keyboard again and again, so he could hear the different sounds. "You see, love, that's music," she said. "That's part of God's language."

Leslie seemed to enjoy music more and more. He often sat listening to records or radio for hours, head down, serious, intense, a study in concentration.

Sometimes his foot or hand even moved methodically with the beat.

Then, in his sixteenth year, something May calls "The Miracle" occurred.

The family had been in bed for hours. About 3:00 A.M. May awoke and thought she heard music. Assuming that Joe had left the television on, she got up to turn it off. But when she walked into the living room, the television was dark and silent. The music was coming from Leslie's bedroom.

She opened the door and saw her son sitting at the piano, playing Tchaikovsky's Piano Concerto No. 1. The music was Liberace's theme song, and he had heard it numerous times on television.

Leslie had never played a note of music in his life, but now he was playing like a professional, racing up and down the keys, never missing a note, as if he'd been practicing for years.

May fell down on her knees and cried. And laughed. And cried again. She ran for Joe. They were both on their knees for most of the night, praising God and thanking Him for giving their boy the gift of music. At last, God had given him a talent. And what a wonderful talent!

Amazingly, Leslie still could not walk alone. He had never gotten out of bed by himself before. Yet somehow he had slid out of his bed and pulled himself up on the piano bench and begun to play.

The next morning May called friends, neighbors, Leslie's doctor—everybody she could think of—to tell them about Leslie's amazing talent. They all came to listen and found the impromptu concerts both magnificent and incredible. Impulsively May taped Leslie at the keyboard and played the tapes outdoors so that all the world could hear what "my helpless, spastic son" had become.

Leslie began to play everything he heard: classics, hymns, marches, ragtime, ballads. He amazed his mother by playing many of the old English songs that she had sung earlier to him. From then on everything that Leslie heard, he could repeat. May began to be more selective about what he listened to. She bought good records by accomplished artists, so that her son would hear nothing but the best music.

Although Leslie's palsied hands could not yet hold a cup or pick up a piece of food, they were relaxed and controlled when he played the piano. They moved decisively, the long fingers gliding gracefully. His timing was good; his interpretation powerful. Playing the piano, Leslie Lemke was in his own special world—a world he loved, a world where all of his senses came alive.

He obviously enjoyed performing and disliked having to stop. He never seemed to tire and never ran out of the endless selections that he was storing up every day. The dozens of songs in his repertoire grew to hundreds, then thousands, until nobody knew how many pieces he could play at will.

Joe and May had to have the piano moved out of Leslie's bedroom and onto the porch to make room for all the people who were coming to hear him.

The neighborhood children, who had stopped visiting when Leslie showed no response as a baby, began to come again, asking Leslie to play all their favorite songs. Sometimes as many as ten or twelve youngsters crowded around him, each interrupting the other with requests.

Visitors came and played some little-known piece,

then reacted with disbelief when Leslie played it right back to them, often in a different key. There seemed to be no music that Leslie could not repeat and remember. He needed only to hear it once.

Word spread all over Pewaukee that Leslie had received his gift and May her miracle. And May's prayers changed from prayers of supplication to expressions of thanksgiving. Instead of asking God for help, she was thanking him for a miracle.

"Oh, thank You, thank You, dear God," she praised. "I asked for a gift, but I didn't expect anything so big! You really brought me to my knees! Thank You for the wonderful thing you have done for Leslie!"

The miracle was only the beginning. After that night of Tchaikovsky, all kinds of things began to happen.

Chapter 8

Growing

May noticed that Leslie's thin, frail body was changing. Instead of looking like a withered child, he was filling out, looking less like a boy and more like a man. He was nearly seventeen, and he was growing so fast that he would soon be as tall as Joe. Although he was thin, he weighed well over a hundred pounds. His hands, his body, his senses all seemed to be coming alive, suddenly springing out of their lethargy.

He was not walking alone, but May noticed that each day he walked a little faster, a little steadier along the fence. His hands grew raw and blistered from gripping the fence too hard, so she bought him a pair of gloves.

In the next few years she bought Leslie *dozens* of pairs of gloves. He gripped the fence so intensely that in no time at all, the gloves were in shreds. Leslie spent more and more time walking up and down the fence, enjoying the outdoors, listening to the neighbor children play. He became stronger and stronger until he was nearly running as he held on to the fence.

One hot July afternoon Leslie was going up and down the fence when a boy of about fourteen called to him from the road that passed the house. He stood by the fence and began to tease Leslie.

"How fast can you travel up that fence?"

"What's your name, or can't you talk?"

May came flying out the back door in a rage. (Leslie was never out of her sight for long.) "What do you think you're doing, mister?" she screamed. "You're annoying the child, and he can't even defend himself! You should be out doing something for these kinds of people, not teasing or making fun of them. You might have one of your own someday. These children need to be loved and protected, not tormented!"

Concern for Leslie was always foremost in May's mind. Later that summer she looked down at the lake one morning and said to Joe, "I think we ought to have a fence built between the house and lake. One of these days that boy is going to end up in the water."

So they had another fence built to enclose the back yard, giving Leslie plenty of walking space.

May reasoned that if Leslie was able to hold onto the fence and walk outdoors, couldn't he hang onto her and walk indoors? They tried it, and it worked. Leslie learned to put both hands on May's shoulders and shuffle along behind. Soon, instead of carrying him or trailing him with a belt, May walked her son to his bedroom, to the piano, to his chair.

Joe retired the year Leslie was seventeen, so May

had more help with the boy. If one of them had to shop or run errands, the other could stay home with Leslie.

With Joe home, May also thought the time had come to teach Leslie to go to the bathroom by himself. "After all, he can walk with us now, Joe," she said. "So maybe you can teach him." All the years that Leslie couldn't walk, May had relied on a bedpan for her son. "What a wonderful thing it would be, Joe, if he could be like other boys."

Joe took over the bathroom training and proved he was every bit as patient as May. There were several months of constant observation and surveillance, but eventually, Leslie began to catch on. And May happily threw out the bedpan.

Next May tried to teach Leslie to walk by hanging onto the furniture. But he seemed frightened and unsure of himself if May or Joe were not right there with him. Patiently May decided to let him walk along with her for a while longer until he felt secure. Eventually she taught him to feel his way around the house.

Meanwhile the Lemkes' life fell into a comfortable routine again. No more having to carry Leslie to the store, no more dragging him down to the lake for water exercises, no more standing him by the fence to watch him fall in a heap, no more bedpans to clean.

After breakfast Leslie went to the bathroom and May dressed him. Then she took him to the piano, where he played for an hour or so. Next she or Joe helped him to the fence for some exercise and fresh air.

After lunch May walked him to his favorite chair in

the living room and played records for him while he rested. Sometimes he took a nap. After resting he played the piano again. Then May or Joe took him back outside for more exercise until dinner.

With Leslie responding, May sensed an even greater challenge to discover new things for him to do. One day she bought a large ball and took Leslie out in the backyard, sitting him on a chair. She let him feel the ball, then she bounced it up and down, letting him hear the sound of it.

"I'm going to throw the ball to you, love," she explained. "It will make a sound like a swishing noise when it goes through the air. Now, you try to catch it."

May was astounded. Leslie caught the ball every time. He clearly was enjoying the activity and apparently could hear the ball coming through the air. "His ears must be magnificent!" she said to Joe that evening.

May had another idea. As Leslie continued to play the piano his fingers were becoming stronger and more agile. His eighteenth birthday came and went. "Why can't he learn to eat and drink by himself?" she asked Joe one evening. "Even with the palsy, I bet he could learn to hold a cup or pick up a piece of meat."

She began this new series of lessons with a tiny bit of milk in a plastic cup. Patiently, slowly, May showed him how to hold the cup with both hands and raise it to his mouth. Leslie picked up the cup, banged it on the table, and milk splashed all over his face.

"No, no, love. That milk is to drink!" May said over and over again in the next few days. Then she carefully showed him again how to hold the cup and lift it to his mouth so he could drink by himself.

May noticed that Leslie seemed to be listening more to what she was saying. Often, he turned his head toward her as she spoke or reached his hand toward her. He seemed to be trying to understand.

She gave Leslie the cup again. He banged it on the table. May was pleased that he was getting so much movement. "No, no, love," she said. "That's beautiful, but that's not the way to do it." And she showed him once more.

A few weeks later Leslie finally held the cup by himself and raised it to his mouth. But instead of drinking, he blew—hard—and the milk ran down his clothes. Again, with infinite patience, May responded, "No, no, love. Not like that. You don't blow it out. You drink it down."

Since nothing else seemed to work, May put a little sugar in the milk and a little more on the rim of the cup. The trick worked. Leslie liked the sugar, and the milk began to go down.

Her success at teaching Leslie to drink by himself gave May confidence that she could teach him to eat. She put a few bite-sized pieces of food on his plate. "Now love, I'm going to teach you to eat by yourself," she said.

She placed his fingers in the dish so he could feel the food. Leslie put his face down close to the dish and tried to suck the food up like milk. "Good for you, baby," May said. "One of these days you're going to eat right."

Day after day she offered Leslie a few bits of food on the plate. Slowly he figured out that pushing the pieces into his mouth with his fingers was easier than sucking them in. He still bent his face close to the plate, but he managed to scrape everything in. When he was finished, he wiped the plate with his fingers and licked them clean.

Gradually May taught Leslie to pick up a piece of food and put it into his mouth. His hand trembled—the procedure was clearly an effort for him—but soon he could eat almost all his food unassisted. Because of the palsy he could not manage a fork or spoon. But he rarely spilled anything or made a mess. He scraped his plate clean, licked his fingers, and obviously enjoyed eating.

Chapter 9

New Sounds

May began to wonder why Leslie could not talk. He never even made a sound. If he could hear, why was he unable to talk? She gently put two fingers into his mouth one day and moved his tongue around. All of a sudden Leslie made a gurgling noise. "You see," she said to him, "that shows you *can* make a noise."

She moved his tongue again and told him, "This is your tongue, and you use it for eating. But you can use it for talking, too."

She put his hands to her own lips, then put a piece of apple in her mouth. "Now I'm eating," she explained. In a few moments she put his hands to her lips. "Now, you see, love, I'm talking." She put her mouth against his cheek and sang a song. "Now I'm singing. Isn't it amazing how many things you can do with your mouth?"

Often when Leslie played the piano, May sat beside him, pressing her mouth against his cheek, singing the words to him. She explained to Joe, "Maybe I can teach him to talk by touch. When you touch someone's face or arm, you are showing affection— how you care about them. Maybe if I keep at it, I can get him to talk."

May worked every day, talking and singing into Leslie's cheek, moving his tongue, touching his lips, trying to get him to understand and to make some small effort toward language.

The only response was a flat, guttural grunt. *What else can I try?* she kept asking herself. *Maybe there's a clinic somewhere where they can teach him to talk.*

Maybe I'll call my doctor and ask, she was musing one day, when she became aware of a strange sound in the house.

What was that? She stopped washing dishes, hands poised in midair, in order to hear better. The sound was *singing*. Leslie was playing the piano, but who was singing? She tried to think where Joe was. *He went to the bank. He can't be back yet.* She knew the radio wasn't on. Nor was the television. Besides, this wasn't a trained voice. It sounded kind of flat, kind of throaty—like Leslie's.

"Leslie!" She ran to the porch. He was singing a song that Frank Sinatra had made popular—"I Did It My Way." The words were muffled and hesitant, but *Leslie was singing*.

May fell to her knees again. "Oh, God," she prayed. "Another miracle. Now I know why you put Leslie on this earth: to sing and play for people. Oh, thank You, God! Thank You!" She wept anew in gratitude for another gift, another miracle, another talent.

Leslie was nineteen years old when he started singing. He had never spoken a word.

From then on Leslie sang along with much of his music. At first his singing was indistinct, occasionally missing phrases. His tongue seemed to get in the way, twisting sounds rather than caressing or honing them. But like a child learning to talk, Leslie's voice developed and matured until at twenty, he had a strong, rich baritone. The talent added another remarkable dimension to his emerging personality. As he listened to music he recorded both melody and words in his brain.

One summer day when Leslie was twenty-two, he was walking up and down the fence, singing an Irish song at the top of his voice. A half hour later, a man came walking up the road and knocked on the door. "I heard someone singing a beautiful Irish song," he said when May answered. "Do you know who it was?"

May explained that he was her son who was blind and retarded.

"Oh, what a beautiful voice," he said. "We just moved in, and I thought there must be another Irishman living around here."

Despite the range of Leslie's repertoire, May loved hearing Leslie sing the old songs she used to sing to him most of all: old English ballads, World War I songs, and her favorite hymns. Sometimes, she even joined him in a duet.

May was fixing dinner late one afternoon when she heard Leslie playing something she had never heard him play. She stopped a moment and listened. Suddenly her eyes welled up with tears. The music was the first song she had sung to him as a baby. She had changed the words from "two lovely eyes" to "without any eyes."

Only a baby small,
Dropped from the skies.
Only a baby small,
Without any eyes.
Only a baby small,
Never at rest.
Small, but how dear to me,
God knows best.

Three years passed. Leslie was nearly twenty-six years old.

May had more questions, new expectations. "If he can sing, then why can't he talk?" she asked Joe one evening. "Words are words, whether they're spoken or sung."

She began again with the method she knew, pressing her lips against his cheek, forming words and talking through his cheek. She thought if he could hear the sounds and feel her lips, he might get the idea. The technique had worked before. He certainly was singing beautifully. Again May worked long hours for weeks, then months, trying to get Leslie to form words—moving his tongue, touching her lips, trying to get him to understand.

One day the following summer May was planting petunias while Leslie walked up and down the fence, listening to the three children next door. They were playing in the yard, and occasionally they called out to Leslie.

"Hi, Leslie. Are you having fun?"

"Hey, you're almost running today!"

"We heard you singing last night, Leslie."

Then they went back to their play.

May, too, engaged in one-sided conversation with her son.

"These petunias are beautiful, Leslie. Some are pink, some a lovely lavender. I'm going to plant my Easter lily to see if it will bloom. Are you too warm, Leslie? Shall I take your shirt off? School's out now, you know. You'll be able to hear the children all summer. Won't that be fun? And what are you doing now, love?"

"I'm having fun." The voice was flat, mechanical, unfamiliar. May looked up. *Who said that? Is one of the children being silly and trying to confuse me?*

"I'm having fun." There was no question this time. The children were down by the lake, playing in the boat. It was Leslie! He wasn't singing those words. *He was talking.*

"Oh, God! Oh, God!" May said as she looked at her son. "Now You have given him words so he can speak. I'm overcome with joy. Thank You from me! Thank You from Leslie! Thank You, God!" Exhausted with emotion, she fell to her knees.

Leslie continued to talk, on and off, very primitively at first. With practice, his words became more distinct, his sentences more complete. He was unable to carry on a conversation, but he could respond to simple questions. He began to repeat what he heard: television commercials, thoughts that May had spoken to him. He called Joe "Daddy" and referred to May as "Honey-love." He could tell people what his name was and who his parents were.

May had read to Leslie since he was a small boy—stories about the sun, moon, and stars, stories about Jesus, about nature—topics she thought might interest him. When they spent time outside, she tried to explain these things to him.

As Leslie talked, the ideas and concepts that May

had read to him came back to her through him. One evening Joe told Leslie that the moon was out. Leslie startled his parents by saying, "Yes, that silvery light is shining through the window."

"And where did you hear that?" May asked.

"I can see it," Leslie replied.

"You know, Joe, maybe he 'sees' more than we think he does," May said, reflectively. "How do we know what's going on inside his head?"

The following two years were filled with new accomplishments for Leslie—feeling his way around the house, brushing his teeth, bathing and dressing by himself. There were also new experiences—flying to Arizona, taking overnight trips, attending weddings.

May and Joe provided motivation and encouragement. Leslie came up with the courage to try.

Leslie began to tell stories to May. His voice still had a flatness about it, with little intonation or expression. But he seemed to enjoy communicating and being part of a conversation.

"I guess I'm going to a wedding," he said to May one morning. May's granddaughter was to be married the following April. "They're going to have a big wedding cake and some cool lemon juice," Leslie went on. "And Mary's going to be there. And I'm going to play the piano."

Later that day May said to Joe, "Leslie's got the whole wedding planned, and I don't even have an invitation yet!"

One winter evening, the family was sitting around the living room in front of a crackling fire. Leslie was slumped in his favorite chair as usual.

"What is that sniffing I hear?" May looked around and realized that the sound was coming from Leslie. "What is it, love?"

"I'm crying," he said matter-of-factly. Leslie knew what crying was because he had heard May cry and had felt her tears, but neither May nor Joe had ever seen Leslie cry. Leslie reached up to his own face this time, feeling his own tears. And then he began to sob, his whole body shaking.

He couldn't tell his parents why he was crying. "Oh, Joe," May said, "it's like a river, like something that has been inside of him all his life. I think he's crying a lifetime of misery—of pure agony!"

Finally Leslie was calm once more. Neither May nor Joe have seen him cry since.

May decided Leslie should walk alone—this time, for sure. After all, he was six feet tall and weighed one hundred fifty pounds. He wasn't a boy any longer; he was a man. Although he resisted losing the security of their shoulders, May was firm. "You can't walk this way forever. You've got to start feeling your way around the house by yourself now."

Again, she took him from room to room, putting his hands on furniture, mantles, and windowsills, showing him objects he could hold onto. They explored the house together many, many times. May pointed out doorways, chairs, plants, and dressers so that Leslie was familiar with the minutest details. She guided his hands from doorway to chair, chair to sofa, showing him how he could move around by himself.

He was slow and cautious at first, and very uneasy. Sometimes he couldn't find the window ledge or the doorknob and he would call out, "Honey-love!" Other times he simply uttered some indistinguishable sound of frustration. Yet, each day his body relaxed a little more, and he moved with greater assurance.

In a few weeks he was capable of walking throughout the house by himself: to the kitchen, to the bathroom, wherever he wanted to go. He called out his destinations loud enough for Joe and May to hear.

"I think I'm going to play the piano now."

"I'm going to sit in my chair."

"I'm on my way to the bathroom."

His voice was still mechanical and buried deep in his throat, but his body showed confidence and pride. No longer did he have to ask May or Joe for help. He could get around by himself.

About a month after Leslie had become adept at moving around the house, May heard a commotion in the living room. She poked her head in and there was Leslie, feeling his way around the room, moving in circles.

"Whatever are you doing, love?" May asked, a bit puzzled.

"I'm exercising," Leslie replied. From then on, "exercise" was a part of Leslie's regimen. Whether he walked up and down the fence or circled the living room, it was always the same. He was "exercising."

"Leslie should begin taking care of himself," May said to Joe one evening. "I'll teach him to brush his teeth and dress himself. I do wish we had a bathtub so Leslie could sit and scrub himself." The Lemkes' tiny facilities had room only for a shower.

"I've got it!" May said, after a few minutes. "Why don't we have a tub built into the shower? Couldn't they just weld it in, Joe? You'd just need a little dip in front to step over."

May does have ideas, Joe thought to himself. *She's always thinking of something!*

After being told by several welders that the idea would never work, the Lemkes found a man who said he would do it. He took the measurements of the shower stall and arrived a week later with a three-foot-high tub that fit perfectly. He welded it to the frame, and the tub sat inside the stall, exactly as May had imagined.

"It's perfect," she said excitedly. "Now, Leslie can sit in the water and enjoy his bath like other children."

May filled the tub the next morning after breakfast and helped Leslie over the edge, into the warm water. Cautiously, he held onto the side and felt the water, splashing a little to get used to it. Each time May helped him into the water, he grew a little bolder until he was splashing grandly and putting his head under, having a wonderful time.

"I'm going to my adventure bath," Leslie said whenever he heard May filling the tub. "Robin and Batman are coming in, too."

"He always talks to Robin and Batman when he's in the tub," May told Joe over lunch. "He must have heard them on TV."

A few months later, May had the welder return to install a pull-down shower so Leslie could wash and rinse his hair.

The next lesson for Leslie was how to brush his teeth. When he first tried, he brushed so hard that his gums bled.

"No, no, love," May said encouragingly. "That's

too hard. Be more gentle." May went out and bought new brushes with the softest bristles she could find. She took away the toothpaste because he tried to eat it. Instead she gave him a bowl of clean, warm water to rinse his brush in. Slowly he learned to brush up and down more gently, and May was satisfied.

Learning to dress himself took a little more time. Because of the palsy he had poor muscle control; consequently, getting a shirt over his head, pulling up a pair of pants, or slipping on socks and shoes took a long time. But Leslie worked hard at the tasks, and May was always there to give him a hand if he became frustrated. He learned to feel the labels on his clothing to tell the front from the back. The last thing that Leslie learned was to fasten a button. May replaced many of the buttons on his clothing with larger sizes and enlarged the buttonholes so that Leslie could manage them himself.

The more Leslie accomplished, the more he structured his own life. He sensed when nine o'clock came every evening and rose from his chair to announce, "I'm going to bed now." Before the Lemkes knew it, he had undressed, said his prayers, and was fast asleep.

He said his prayers aloud, reciting a litany all his own: the Lord's Prayer, followed by prayers from his church and churches where he had visited. To close, he prayed for all the people he knew.

May taught Leslie a prayer that seemed to speak for his own existence. He liked to recite it for visitors.

> *Dear Lord,*
> *I hold in my thoughts today*
> *The good health and happy things*

I wish in my own future.
I call upon the limitless power
Of my Creator.
My body expresses that power.
                              Amen.

Leslie's morning routine was as predictable as bedtime. At seven o'clock he got up, went to the bathroom, dressed himself, and arrived in the kitchen for breakfast.

As Leslie's progress continued, the special times—birthdays, Christmas, visits with relatives—took on more significance.

On his birthday, January 31, Leslie always had his favorite cake, topped with whipped cream and strawberries. As he matured he appreciated more fully the gifts of candy, clothing, books, or records.

Weddings and church services were an adventure, because Leslie always assumed he was there to play the piano. At one family wedding the friends and relatives were going through the receiving line when they heard music—loud music! Nobody knew how Leslie had done it, but he had found a piano and was playing and singing at the top of his voice.

By 1975 the Lemkes felt confident enough to fly with Leslie to Arizona, to visit May's son and family. May and Joe prepared Leslie for the flight by explaining how he would be going up in the air. It might feel strange at times, they warned. Leslie was a model passenger, enjoying the snacks and the special attention he received from the stewardesses.

When they landed and were met by May's son, Leslie said, "Oh, it was awful! We were thirty thousand feet in the air!"

"He heard the pilot say that," May laughed. "That boy doesn't miss anything!"

Leslie was reluctant when May took him to the strange bed in her son's home that night.

"This isn't my bed," he told his mother.

"No, love, this isn't your bed." She took his hands and let him feel the mattress. "But we're visiting now, and you've got to get used to another bed. So just do like you do at home. Take off your clothes, get into your pajamas, and go to bed." Leslie obediently went to bed and fell asleep at once.

During their visit they decided to go shopping in Mexico on a Sunday morning. Shortly before they reached the border, May saw a tiny church on a hill. "Let's stop there and go to church," she suggested.

They drove up to the church to find that it was filled with Indians and Mexicans. May asked the minister if he would like to have a blind and retarded boy play and sing for his people.

"I'd be delighted," the minister said. "These people don't speak much English, but they sure know what music is!" The minister led Leslie to the piano, and he played a few hymns. The people sat spellbound, tears rolling down their faces.

When the service was over, people congregated around the Lemkes to thank them for coming. An old Indian woman approached May shyly. "I haven't been to church in twenty years," she said in broken English, "but something kept telling me to come today." She reached out and took May's hands in her own. "I'm so glad I came today, my dear lady, because I feel like I've just seen a miracle."

The Lemkes also began taking Leslie out to eat occasionally. Knowing that some people are offended by disabled people, May frequently made a public announcement before they sat down.

"Folks," she said, "I'd like to talk to you a few minutes. I have brought a blind, spastic, and retarded boy here today. He has to eat with his fingers, and he has every right to eat his own way. That's the only way he can learn to do things for himself. I have to feed him occasionally, but he's very polite, and he eats and drinks nicely. He never spills anything, and he won't annoy any of you. But if you think it will bother you, you might rather sit across the room."

There were times when she had to take Leslie in the ladies room; she simply made a similar announcement and walked on in. "You'll have to excuse me, ladies," she called out, "but I'm bringing in a blind, unfortunate boy who needs a little help."

One fall evening in 1980 Joe and May were sitting by the lake, reminiscing over the years.

"Think of it, May. In a few months Leslie will be twenty-nine," Joe mused.

"Do you remember what he looked like, Joe? You know, the day the nurse brought him."

They were both silent, locked together in the memory of that helpless, forlorn-looking infant. "He's going to die anyway," the nurse had said so matter-of-factly. "He's going to die. How could anything live, looking like that?"

May suddenly straightened. Enough looking back. She learned long ago not to look back. If she let herself live in the past, she'd go crazy. The war, the explosion, the deaths, leaving her mother, the fire, the tornado. You have to put those things out of your mind.

"Joe!"

Now Joe sat up. "What is it, May?"

"Leslie's not through learning yet, you know." Her old voice was back, with the familiar high, sharp staccato. "I've got a lot more things planned for him. I want to teach him to spell, to print his name, to open a door by himself, to get in a car. . . ." She went on and on.

Joe smiled to himself. "Do you really think he can do all those things, May?"

"Well, we can't give up, you know. How do we know what might come next?"

She looked up at the sky. It was clear, with a full moon and a panorama of stars.

"It's like waiting for Jesus," she said. "We don't know when He's coming, but we never quit waiting for Him. It's that way with Leslie. We don't know when it's coming, or what's coming. But we know it always does, don't we, Joe?"

Chapter 10

The Savant Syndrome

While Leslie enthralled me with his musical precocity, he also piqued my interest in his rare, somewhat elusive condition known by the unfortunate name *idiot savant*. The term, which originated in France about seventy-five years ago, is an irritant to readers, viewers, and parents of the retarded—including May Lemke, as I soon discovered.

When the term appeared in my *Milwaukee Journal* story on the Lemkes, one annoyed reader wrote:

> The Journal's beautiful story on Leslie Lemke, the brain-damaged boy who plays music by ear, was spoiled by only one thing—a psychiatrist's characterization of Leslie's condition as "idiot savant."
>
> Why is it that doctors cannot see how cruel and prejudicial it is to use such terms as "mongolism" instead of "Down's syndrome," or "gargoylism" instead of "Hurler's or Hunter's syndrome," or "idiot" instead of "brain-damaged" or "retarded?"

I decided to visit Dr. Darold Treffert, the psychiatrist who had been the source of my story. We had talked only by telephone, and I wanted to know more about Leslie's condition, more than a simple definition.

Face to face with Dr. Treffert, I found a trim, casually dressed young man who looked as if he had just graduated from medical school. I discovered he had been practicing psychiatry for twenty years.

"Can't we call this phenomenon something besides *idiot savant?*" I began. "That term is extremely offensive, you know, to parents of retarded children."

He nodded in agreement. "It's an unfortunate term. I'm all in favor of dropping it for *savant syndrome*. The word *savant* means 'knowledgeable,' and the term is used to describe a person who has an area of subnormal intelligence with spectacular islands of intelligence. In other words, that person likely will display unusual aptitudes or brilliance in some special field, incongruous with the rest of his mental abilities."

Dr. Treffert told me that only a handful of such cases are reported in scientific literature, although obviously all cases have not been written up. Neither have they been studied in any depth, he added, although it has been established that male savants far outnumber females.

"What kind of skills do they have?" I asked. "Are they all musical or do they have other abilities?"

"Most often, they excel in either mathematics or music," Dr. Treffert explained, "but other talents show up as well." He listed some specific skills: calendar calculation (the ability to tell the day of the week of a particular date in any year), mathematical computation (usually done without paper and pencil with amazing rapidity), sensational powers of recall, mechanical ability, and exceptional ability in art.

He cited some cases he had observed in his own practice over the years. One was a boy who could calculate exactly where to stand for shots in basketball. He was able to throw the ball endlessly and rarely miss a basket. "Some professional basketball team could have used him!" Dr. Treffert said, laughing.

Then there was the boy who studied the Milwaukee bus schedule until he had it memorized. "If you told him the time of day and the bus number, he could tell you the corner where you would be standing to catch that particular bus," Dr. Treffert related.

"Why did he pick a bus schedule to memorize?" I asked. "Could he have done the same thing with an encyclopedia or a dictionary?"

"That's one of the things we don't know. Maybe it was happenstance—he just picked up the right piece of literature and really zeroed in."

Dr. Treffert went on to describe a case of mathematical manipulation. This particular savant could stand in front of a fast-moving train and add the numbers of the cars instantly. He came up with the correct total every time.

Later, at the library, I read of a case where a man used this same ability in a different way. He was taken to the theater and later stunned his host by commenting, not on the performance, but on the exact number of words spoken by the actors and the number of steps taken by the dancers.

I spent most of an afternoon on that trip to the library, poring over some fascinating studies of this small but remarkable psychological group.

I found that two of the most publicized savants are identical twins named Charles and George (last

names were not included) who, although clearly retarded in most areas, are geniuses when it comes to
calendar calculations. They can rattle off the years in
which a given date will fall on a Sunday or which
month in a given year commences on a Monday.
They can identify in almost an instant the day of the
week for dates as far in the future as A.D. 7000 or for
dates hundreds of years in the past.

I also read of a Boston woman who was tested in
1970 and found to have phenomenal music history
abilities. She could identify the period in which virtually any piece of music was written and play any
composer's tune as if it had been written by another,
in addition to reciting extensive information about
music *per se*.

Few savants have managed to use their talents to
become self-supporting. One who did is a Japanese
artist named Yoshihiko Yamamoto. Despite an IQ of
40 and speech and hearing impairments, Yamamoto
has become a nationally known artist.

I had more questions for Dr. Treffert. "What causes
this strange phenomenon? Where do savants get this
spectacular island of intelligence that we're talking
about?"

"Again, we don't know enough about the human
mind to really understand the phenomenon," Dr.
Treffert responded, "but several theories have been
explored in an attempt to explain its existence."

He pointed out that one of the most recent theories
concerns the dominant and nondominant hemi-
spheres of the brain. According to this hypothesis, in
savants the dominant hemisphere of the brain has
been affected, while the nondominant hemisphere

has been left relatively intact. The dominant (the left hemisphere in a right-handed person) measures intelligence, verbal skills, and speech; the nondominant is associated with music and abstract ability.

Another theory suggests that savant syndrome is the result of a selective area of the brain being spared from the injury that caused the general loss of mental capacity. Either through constant exercise of this one functioning area, or perhaps because it is the only area to receive and process outside sensations normally, its ability to perform is greatly enhanced. The principle is the same as in a blind person who has developed extraordinary hearing to compensate for lack of sight.

Organic factors play an important role in the latter theory. Currently, some psychologists are looking outside environmental influences for the pieces to the puzzle of the brain's protein chemistry.

In my reading on the savant syndrome I had come across the expression *computer brain* several times. I thought of Leslie hearing a song once and recording it instantly in his memory. I thought of the hundreds, perhaps even thousands, of songs that he can recall instantly and play.

I asked Dr. Treffert if he thought computer brain an apt description.

"Normally man has a phenomenally creative and abstractive ability," he replied. "We can create, we can abstract, we can think, we can dream, but we have a very poor memory. A computer has a phenomenal memory, but that's all it is. When we refer to a computer brain, we're saying that the brain develops greatly in the area of memory, but it never broadens the scope of its abilities. There is depth, but little breadth.

"The savant syndrome is characterized by a narrowing down—a funneling effect—of the kind of abilities that get deeper but never spread. There is very little generalization of those abilities. This is, of course, in sharp contrast to a normal genius, who has intellectual abilities in many areas and talent spread over a broad spectrum."

Dr. Treffert explained that people like Leslie, with exceptional musical ability, are unable to learn to play their instruments by reading music.

"What about people who learn music by ear?" I asked. "They don't read music, either."

"But they can if they choose to," Dr. Treffert said. "Playing by ear is a talent, like knowing how to draw, but people with that talent also can learn to read music. A savant can't."

I was always intrigued by the way Leslie listened to music. Sometimes he looked as if he were sleeping. Other times he assumed an expression of great seriousness. Often he shielded his eyes or face with one hand. What would have been distractions for others did not bother him.

One afternoon I took my children to visit the Lemkes. Lynn, my oldest daughter, played a song that Leslie had never heard. While she played and Leslie listened, the rest of us in the room continued our conversation, making no effort to lower our voices. When Lynn was finished, Leslie moved over to the piano and played the same piece. With *no* mistakes!

"In all my years of practice," Dr. Treffert said, "I have never come across a case with such an incredible musical ability. What makes it even more striking is that Leslie is also blind and suffers from cerebral palsy."

It occurred to me that I had been so involved researching the savant syndrome condition, I almost had overlooked the cerebral palsy.

I read in my medical encyclopedia that cerebral palsy is a condition that affects the brain centers having to do with muscular control, *cerebral* meaning "brain-centered" and *palsy* meaning "paralysis." People with cerebral palsy have a great deal of trouble controlling their muscles. They sometimes are afflicted with chorea (involuntary jerking movements) or a slow, writhing type of constant movement, chiefly in the fingers, along with poor sense of balance, tremor, and spastic muscles.

I tried to relate the definition to Leslie. He has a poor sense of balance and muscle spasms. He still can't walk more than a step or two alone without grasping for something to hang onto. Maneuvering food or a cup to his mouth requires a great deal of concentration and effort, and he is unable to use a fork or spoon. He is also unable to use a cane or to learn braille.

I talked with Dr. Rona Alexander, director of a cerebral palsy project in Milwaukee. She said classifying specifically the type of cerebral palsy Leslie has is very difficult without evaluating him. There is a considerable range in both the severity and the symptoms of cerebral palsy. It is not a single condition, but rather a group of conditions with a common denominator: some form of injury to motor control centers in the brain.

"What are the causes of cerebral palsy?" I asked.

She listed a few possibilities: birth injuries, infections of the mother and the embryo, problems in natural development. "But the causes really haven't been established, except for the fact that there is always some cut-off of oxygen to the brain, causing brain damage," Dr. Alexander added.

I was surprised to learn that the incidence of cerebral palsy has decreased significantly in the past twenty years. "What is responsible for this?" I asked.

"Partly the development of the rubella vaccine, which virtually has eliminated German measles, a common cause of cerebral palsy," Dr. Alexander explained. "Other factors are better prenatal care, improved neonatal conditions, more sophisticated equipment, better nutrition, and greater understanding of drugs."

I told Dr. Alexander how May had warned me not to come on too strong the first time I met Leslie.

"Absolutely true," she said. "Many cerebral palsied people are hypersensitive to stimulation. They should be approached slowly in order that they may be forewarned. When touching or shaking their hand, a firm, slow, steady kind of touch is recommended—not so light that it tickles but firm enough to give them some feeling.

"Body placement also can be threatening to a person with cerebral palsy. We suggest not approaching the person too fast or leaning over them. Because of Leslie's blindness, a person really ought to speak first before approaching him."

One of the things I had noticed about Leslie in the year I had known him was the improvement in his speech. "When I first met Leslie," I said to Dr. Treffert one afternoon, "his vocabulary consisted of yes and no. But now he answers many of the questions I ask. He seems to be developing a larger vocabulary and to be answering more intelligently."

Dr. Treffert agreed that from what May had described, a generalization had been occurring with Leslie in the past year. "His abilities do seem to be spreading out. As I said earlier when we discussed the computer brain, this does not often occur.

"The most logical explanation for this is May Lemke herself. Since most of our savants are in institutions, the care and example of the Lemkes is a rarity."

He used a tripod to demonstrate his point. "You see, for the savant the first leg of the tripod is the limitation. The second leg is an area from which he gets a lot of reinforcement—positive "strokes." In Leslie's case, this area is his music, of course. The third leg, which so often is missing, is a person in that child's life who is motivating—one who will look beyond the limitations to find the one or two areas of intactness or beauty and zero in on them."

Looking beyond the limitations. That phrase reminded me of something I couldn't quite grasp. Then I knew. May had said it one day so matter-of-factly that I always would remember it.

"We've always tried to treat Leslie like a normal child," she said. "Joe and I never worried much about what was wrong with him. We just tried to teach him to do whatever he could do. And whatever he couldn't do, we did."

But Dr. Treffert was speaking. "You know, we have something here that is far beyond an interesting scientific story. This is the incredible story of an amazing woman and her unshakable belief in her foster son. The story of an extraordinary, dedicated mother who, with a great deal of love, concern, care, effort, and patience, has worked with this youngster. It's really a melding of these two circumstances—Leslie's condition and May's care—that makes this story unique."

I half-wondered where Leslie would be today had it not been for May—or May had it not been for Leslie. Strange, I couldn't imagine one without the other. Or the two without Joe—silent, steady, faithful Joe. The balance wheel.

"Without May, Leslie might have been presented as some sort of oddity. But May has turned his story into one of inspiration. She has overshadowed the scientific elements and turned us all into believers.

"She is so enthusiastic, so bubbly, so full of belief that she makes everyone else believe in Leslie. She is also very humble. She says, 'It's not me. It's Leslie.' That's what motivation is all about. You can't motivate anybody without believing in them. When you do believe in them, you cause them to believe in themselves.

"This case ought to be presented as a scientific study somewhere. . . . Yet, maybe it shouldn't be. There is always the risk that scientific analysis might rob it of its beauty. And that would, indeed, be a tragedy."

Chapter 11

The Concert Circuit

It was inevitable that Leslie would one day be led out of his tiny enclosed porch onto the concert stage. But six years passed—years of playing and singing for visitors who came to the Lemke home as well as performances at nursing homes, hospitals, and churches—before his first formal concert in 1974.

Leslie's first recitals were held right on the porch of the Lemke home. Word spread quickly throughout the small community that something had happened on Pewaukee Lake. Friends, ministers, doctors, children, and townspeople hurried over to see and hear May Lemke's "miracle."

One day an old man came to the door and asked if Leslie could sing "The Old Rugged Cross." The time was close to Easter. May invited him in, and Leslie played the hymn.

Tears streamed down the old man's face. As he left, he said, "If God ever showed His presence, it was here today, hearing that boy sing."

On one of their hospital visits, a nurse came down to the central lounge. She had been tending a patient who was going to die, and he wished to see Leslie. They brought the man in on a long stretcher and moved him right up next to the piano. He asked Leslie to sing "A Closer Walk With Thee." When the song was over, the man was crying, and he reached out to hold Leslie's hands.

He died two days later.

Leslie's first public concert, at the 1974 Waukesha County Fair, was more like a "happening." Headlines boasted he drew the largest crowd ever assembled at the county exposition grounds.

I talked about the Lemkes one afternoon with Stance Bergelin, community education coordinator for the Fond du Lac County Department of Social Services. He mentioned attending that first concert.

"What was it like?" I asked. I had read the account in the *Waukesha Freeman* and had wondered if the concert was really all that fantastic.

"It was absolutely incredible!" he said, without a moment's hesitation. "I knew Leslie was retarded and handicapped, but I had no idea how severely until I saw him. He had to be led over to the piano, and he was wobbling, his sense of balance was so bad. He sat kind of slumped over at the keyboard.

"Then his mother spoke to him, and he started to play. It was as if someone had turned on a switch. From the moment he started singing he had the audience in the palm of his hand. The ballads that he sang brought tears to the eyes of the audience. His amazing imitations of Tiny Tim and Louis Armstrong prompted rounds of standing cheers, applause, and laughter.

"The audience absolutely did not want to leave. He had standing ovations after each number and he was brought back for two encores. It was an unbelievable experience."

After the County Fair, the Lemkes continued to perform sporadically for small groups in and around Pewaukee—churches, schools, women's clubs, and civic organizations.

In June of 1980, Stance Bergelin invited the Lemkes to perform at a large, well-publicized benefit for foster parents in Fond du Lac. Like the County Fair in 1974, the concert was another unforgettable evening of applause, encores, and for the first time, television cameras.

"I called a television station, requesting that a reporter and cameraman be sent to the concert," Bergelin recalled. "They agreed to come but made it clear they had only fifteen minutes of shooting time. Once they started interviewing the Lemkes, they got so excited, they stayed for an hour and a half!"

That night marked the Lemkes' foray into television. A brief segment from the concert was shown on the ten o'clock news.

The concert was attended by more than four hundred people, who couldn't get enough of Leslie Lemke.

"When it was over, people just would not leave," Bergelin said. "They gave him a standing ovation. Leslie played more. Another standing ovation. Leslie played again. People wouldn't let him quit! My contract expired at 9:30 p.m., and I almost had to throw people out!"

The more I heard about these Lemke concerts, the more I wanted to go to one. I had been interviewing

May for several weeks, and after our tapings, I always was entertained with a short performance. I had brought my family and a few friends to hear Leslie, but I had not yet attended a real concert, one of those "Evenings With Leslie Lemke."

I learned from May that Leslie's next concert was Sunday night at Atonement Luthern Church in the neighboring town of Muskego.

My husband Lee and I arrived early that night. As we walked into the church vestibule, Lee grabbed my arm and pointed me in the direction of a large bulletin board. "Hey, how about that?" he grinned. "What's it like to be a celebrity?"

There was my story from the *Milwaukee Journal*, and over it, in huge black letters, read the words, *Have you ever seen a miracle? Come and hear Leslie Lemke on Sunday night at 7 P.M.*

Inside the sanctuary we were astounded at how many people were already there. We had to settle for seats near the back. We sat down, joining an audience that was not talking, just waiting. A feeling of expectancy was in the air.

People now were pouring in. The pews were filled, so chairs were hastily assembled for additional seating. Those who came in last had to fend for themselves. The pastor's wife walked onto the platform and told of the amazing Lemkes, May's love and devotion, and the power of God working in their behalf. Then she introduced her guests.

I was wondering where they would enter when something came flying down the aisle, long full skirts swishing and swirling everywhere. Without even looking, I knew May Lemke had arrived. She was waving now, thanking everyone for coming and asking where they were all from in that clipped British accent I had grown to know so well.

Coming along behind in measured steps and utter contrast were Joe and Leslie: Joe in front, walking ever so slowly with Leslie behind, both hands holding on tightly to Joe's shoulders.

The audience rose, almost as one person, slowly and solemnly. Then suddenly, as if the emotions of the crowd had just caught up with the events, the people broke into a thunderous ovation, applauding until Leslie was seated safely at the piano and May obviously was ready to begin. The audience sat down reluctantly, wanting this gesture not to diminish in any way their admiration for the young man who already had won every heart and evoked a good many tears.

While Leslie sat hunched over the piano, waiting quietly, May chattered excitedly about her years with him, what raising him during those years was like and how she had worked with him and prayed for him.

She was a whirlwind in miniature as she dashed around the stage, pointing, pausing, demonstrating—serious for one moment, joking the next. Joe sat quietly in the background while Leslie waited for his cue.

"I believe in Jesus Christ, and I expected Him to do something for Leslie," she was saying. "After all, I prayed to Him over and over again, day after day. I think I was getting to be a real nuisance. 'Lord,' I prayed, 'You said everybody has a talent. Won't you please do something for Leslie? He has no eyes, no voice, no nothing.'

"And after that, the miracle came.

"Play it for them, Leslie," she went on, "what you played that night."

You could hear a collective gasp from the audience as Leslie's fingers struck those first few chords—such fullness of sound, such inexplicable skill. By the end of his powerful, brilliant rendition of Tchaikovsky's piano concerto, we were all believers.

"Well, He finally gave Leslie a gift, didn't He?" May said after the first number. "He really knocked me off my feet. But isn't it wonderful how God answers prayers and takes care of us?

"Now, would you like to hear Leslie do some imitations?" Of course we would. Leslie broke us up with impersonations of Louis Armstrong, Jimmy Durante—and Jeannette McDonald and Nelson Eddy, where he sang *both* parts!

Next he played his own favorites, "I Believe" and "I Was Nobody's Baby But I'm Somebody's Baby Now." He did an Italian aria, a German waltz, an Irish folk tune, and "The Entertainer" from the movie *The Sting*. I looked at the faces around me and saw emotions change as quickly as the tempo: tears to laughter, laughter to looks of incredulity.

"Leslie never needs a microphone," May broke in. "He's such a powerful singer. And you know, you can sing or play anything to him and he'll sing it right back to you, only a whole lot better!

"Who would like to hear something?" she called out.

Hands shot up.

" 'Moonlight Sonata.' "

" 'How Great Thou Art.' "

" 'Hello, Dolly.' "

"*Ave Maria.*"

" 'Bridge Over Troubled Waters.' "

He played them all. "Can you play something by Mozart?" someone asked. "Do you know any marches by John Philip Sousa?" said another. May looked as surprised as anyone when he came up with the right song. One man only hummed a tune. Leslie refreshed his memory—and played the song in full harmony.

A little girl stood up. "Leslie, can you play 'Puff, the Magic Dragon'?" While Leslie played, Joe collected all the kids in the audience and led them through the room in a conga line, up and down the aisles. After that, May told Leslie to perform a couple of commercials for the kids. He mimicked the Electrolux vacuum cleaner ad and a spot for Hush Puppy shoes. The children—young and old—loved it.

May and Joe jumped up and swayed to a couple of waltzes, then May did a solo production while Leslie played a hand-clapping, foot-stomping number. She also enticed the audience into several sing-alongs on some of the old favorites. I had the feeling we were at a good old-time movie, and nobody wanted it to end. I saw no one yawning or looking at their watches or fidgeting in their seats. There was rapt attention all the way.

When May was ready to wrap things up, she had Leslie play his beautiful, highly emotional rendition of "The Lord's Prayer," followed by "God Be With You Till We Meet Again."

Another standing ovation, except this time the applause did not die down. Everyone wanted more. Finally the pastor's wife announced that coffee and cookies were being served in the basement. She also said there was a piano below, so "perhaps Leslie would play a little longer during refreshments." More applause.

When my husband and I joined the crowd in the basement, the Lemkes already were surrounded. Questions were asked that May had answered a hundred times before. "Why were his eyes taken out?" "How can he play the piano that way?" "Where does he learn all those songs?" The questions tumbled all over one another, hopelessly interrupting each other.

After a minute to eat a few cookies, Leslie was led to the piano again. In no time people were crowded three deep, four deep, and more, calling out other requests. Leslie complied, loving every minute of it. Finally May managed to bring the evening to a close, but not without a great deal of reluctance from both Leslie and his admirers.

"What do you think the attraction is?" Lee asked as we got in the car. "Can you explain it?"

"No, I can't," I admitted, "and I've sure never seen anything like it. I've never, *never* seen that kind of emotion—the love that emanated from that audience."

We sat silently for a few moments, lost in our own thoughts. Lee hadn't even started the car.

"Somebody tried to explain it to me once," I offered. "Let's see. I think it was Stance Bergelin, the first time I met him. We were talking about the Lemkes and he said, 'You know, I have worked with Paul Harvey, Robert Schuller, Bob Hope, and many others. But I have never seen people respond the way they do to the Lemkes.

" 'I have sat on that stage with them and seen people really open up. It's as if we finally drop that big guard we all carry around twenty-four hours a day, and we see people for who they are. It's beautiful—beautiful—the way he reaches people. Like anything of value, you can't really explain it. It's like trying to verbalize the beauty of a rose. You just can't do it. That's the way a lot of people feel about Leslie.' "

That made me feel better. *He* couldn't explain it either.

"Lee, Bergelin says another question that often comes up is whether Leslie has any understanding of what he sings. Bergelin and Dr. Treffert discussed that once, and both felt he must have some understanding. Otherwise how could he sing with so much meaning, so much emphasis? When Leslie sings, people *feel* the meaning, the intensity, the emotion of the song. So where does it come from, if not from him?"

I decided to follow up on Leslie's concerts. I soon realized that each was different: a different audience, different requests, different messages from May. The two aspects they all had in common was May's pride in Leslie and May's love for Jesus Christ.

"A lot of you go around saying you're lonely and there's no love in your life," she said to a group of parents. "Then get yourself a foster child or a new baby and you'll have all the love you need. You'll have plenty to keep you busy, too!

"Look at Leslie. Sometimes I have worked twenty-four hours a day with that child. I never left him. I never neglected him, because he needed that love.

"He couldn't let me see it, but how could I know

what was inside of him? We can't ever give up on our handicapped children. Who knows what they can become?"

Then she turned to the subject of institutions, and I saw fire in her eyes.

"We don't need institutions! We need *foster mothers*. Those poor little crippled and retarded children need *mothers* to love them. They need the feel of a mother's body.

"Go into some of those institutions and see the children lying all over the floor, dirty and helpless. Nothing to do. No one to love them. Is this the way we're supposed to treat God's children? Why did He put them on earth? They're here for us to love—a way for us to learn the many lessons we must learn. 'Love ye one another as I have loved you,' Jesus said. If we can show love for these unfortunate children, we can show love to anybody."

Leslie's itinerary at that time included a concert in front of five hundred teenagers. "I can't miss that one," I laughed. "I want to see you handle five hundred kids, May!"

May was more than up to the task. A tiny bundle of energy, she flitted all over the stage.

"Children," she began, with her characteristic bluntness, "I brought you a miracle today: my boy, who is blind, spastic, and retarded. He's going to play and sing for you.

"Look at him and then look at yourselves—how beautiful and talented you are. And just see how much better you can do. There is no need for any of you to be failures. Ever.

"I brought Leslie here because he's never had

much fun in his life. He's never had much of anything. But now he has something, and he's going to give it to you. So let's all join in and sing with him and have a little bit of fun together. Let's make Leslie happy."

The kids loved him. They clapped and sang and stomped and called out requests and had a glorious time.

An opera singer who recently had escaped from Russia by way of Germany happened to be in the audience. He asked to sing a German song for Leslie. When he finished, Leslie, who had never heard the song before, sang it back to him. The kids were astounded, and so was I.

Then the gentleman asked Leslie to sing "The Impossible Dream." Leslie did, and most of us were wiping away the tears.

Of all the concerts Leslie does, I think I like the children's concerts best. The children are so open, so wide-eyed, so spontaneous. At one of these concerts, a small boy asked what had happened to Leslie's eyes, a common question.

"They were scooped right out," May said. "And just think of all the nice things you can see. You can read and write and this boy can't do any of those things. Just think how privileged you are to have a beautiful pair of eyes."

An adorable little girl ran up to May with tears streaming down her face. "Doesn't Leslie have any eyes at all? Can I look?"

May opened one of his eyelids and said, "You see, no eyes at all."

May told the children not to forget to pray for all

the blind children in the world when they said their prayers that night. "And there are many retarded children who can't talk, and crippled children who can't run around," she continued. "We, the able ones, are here on this earth to do like Jesus did. Our duty is to look after them and to love them. That's one reason Jesus came: to teach us to love one another."

At another concert, a child asked, "Well, where is God? I never see Him around."

I found May's answer simple yet eloquent. She held out her hands. "Look at your hands," she said. "There is God's creation. The greatest tool on earth—a pair of hands. The grass growing. That reflects God. The trees and flowers. God is there. The fruit on the trees. There is no place on earth where you can look without seeing God."

May also loves to talk about America to the children. As I think about her own childhood, the war, the hunger, the explosion, tears well up in my eyes.

"You know, children," she said, "I have been in many other countries in my life, but nowhere in the world have I seen a country like America.

"Look at what a wonderful school you have, a wonderful way of living, a mother and father and a nice home. I had a lovely home, too, but the war came along and destroyed it all. I was shipped over to this country to marry a man I'd never met, but he loved me and he was a good man.

"And even when I was left alone, I didn't go around moping. I just went out and did the things I knew I ought to do."

When both parents and children are present, May frequently asks the children if they'd like to sit up front. Many of them do. At a church concert, a little boy went up to the rostrum and asked, "Please, Mrs. Lemke, could Leslie play 'Jesus Loves Me'?"

"Of course he can, dear. And Jesus surely does love you." The child stood awestruck by the piano as Leslie played and sang.

May turned to the three hundred parents who filled the church. "Okay, parents. Now it's your turn. When a little boy can come up like this and say 'Jesus loves me,' I want you all to let him know how much Jesus loves you." So while the boy stood watching, we all sang "Jesus Loves Me." It was a precious moment.

I think one of the most enthusiastic and touching responses the Lemkes have ever received was at the Children's Home in Milwaukee. The children adored Leslie. They were calling out songs, singing, and dancing. May clearly loved and believed in every one of them.

"I wish I could play like Leslie," one small boy said to May. "My mother always wanted me to learn music."

"Then start right here," May said to him emphatically. "Somebody might be able to teach you, and then when you go home you can play and sing for your mother."

When it was time to leave, the children would hardly let them go. They hugged and kissed May until she kidded, "Now children, don't be too rough with me. I have to have something left to get out of here!"

One of them said, "Oh, Mrs. Lemke, please don't go back to Hollywood!"

May burst out laughing. "Hollywood? I've never

been there, and I'm never going. I'm staying right here where I belong!"

I suppose the toughest concert experience for me took place at the Veterans Hospital in Milwaukee. May's own eyes were pools of tears as they wheeled in a number of badly wounded men. When Leslie played the poignant "Over There," I could almost feel the torment going through her.

"Here I am," she said, "a little war baby. I've gone through it, too, so I know something about what you're feeling. I was battered from head to foot in an explosion in England. I wasn't anything to look at, at all."

But this was a concert, not a wake. As soon as May had established her credentials, she switched moods. "We'll push all that aside now. Come on, boys. Tell Leslie what you want to hear. He'll play anything you want!"

As Leslie's reputation grew, so did requests for concerts. With a musical repertoire that included everything from classical to ragtime, there was no group that Leslie could not accommodate. He played for realtors, physicians, senior citizens, conventions, and correctional homes, as well as for weddings and anniversaries.

One of the largest concerts was for two thousand senior citizens in Milwaukee County. Joe Fibeger, organizer of the event, said it was the best attended program ever sponsored for the group. "They swarmed around the piano afterwards, wanting to hear more from that incredible boy. Everyone was talking about the Lemkes. I had chills up and down my spine. It was unbelievable!"

Bob Ripp, a real estate executive, invited the Lemkes to perform for more than three hundred realtors at an annual motivational breakfast.

"Leslie was totally different from any program we had had in the past," Ripp said. "But I had seen him on television and thought, 'If that boy can achieve what he has, each of us has tapped only a fraction of our own potential.' "

Instead of the traditional introduction, Ripp showed tapes of Leslie from a television show. "When I brought him out, there was a standing ovation and not a dry eye anywhere.

"I had it planned how I was going to handle everything. But of course, I had never operated with May Lemke before. The moment I introduced her, I lost control. She was flying all over the stage, hiding behind me, cutting up with the audience, totally in charge. I finally did what everybody else does. I sat back and enjoyed the concert! May never lost the audience for a second. She bowled them over.

"It was the most gloriously successful thing we'd ever done. The impact was tremendous. We always ask for evaluations, but we never got them like we did from that program. People were unable to express their feelings. It was absolutely incredible!"

The Lemkes frequently perform in concerts supporting foster parents, pro-life causes, and handicapped children. Stance Bergelin, who promotes some of these appearances, said, "I invite the Lemkes because I like to show foster parents a real accomplishment. I'm not saying, 'Hey, this can happen to you,' because it's too rare. Most foster parents work terribly hard and see little accomplishment. But I like to show them something that did happen under the most extraordinary circumstances.

"There's no question that the Lemkes are motivating. They seem to instill the belief in people that we can all be better than we are."

May believes strongly in the value of these concerts and will keep them up as long as people want to hear Leslie. "I think it's wonderful that Leslie can sing and play for people. In the dark days, they used to hide these children and never let them out of the house. They need to be noticed, just like normal children. Leslie loves the concerts, and he even loves getting there. He'll say, 'Oh, I'm going out in a car today.'

"There were years and years when he didn't go anyplace. We had to physically carry him everywhere. And now he can enjoy a bit of fun and give a little pleasure to others.

"What Leslie's doing is reaching out and doing God's work. I have scores of letters from people saying that Leslie has brought them closer to Jesus Christ. If you ask Leslie what music means to him, he says it means *love*.

"Everything I do is for Leslie and the retarded children. I don't want anything for myself. Nobody has to pay to see him.

"We're just plain people," she adds, looking at her foster son. "Nothing fancy. We just do what we have to do, don't we, love?"

Chapter 12

On to Television

Producers of Terry Meeuwsen's morning talk show, "A New Day," were busy making preparations for a five-day series of programs recognizing the handicapped. The series was to be called "A Special Week for Special People."

They signed up a physician to talk about adaptive physical education and an attorney to point out the legal rights of the handicapped. Two houseparents were called in to discuss group homes, while a director from Goodwill Industries was asked to describe the employment picture for the handicapped.

Executives from the Association for Retarded Citizens, Special Olympics, and other programs for the handicapped were scheduled to appear. A remote was taped at the office of the *Milwaukee Citizens Newspaper*, a local enterprise staffed with handicapped people. Other remotes were scheduled at Penfield Children's Center, the Curative Rehabilitation Center, and Pleasant View School for retarded children.

Four award-winning athletes from Special Olympics would be interviewed on Friday, the last day of the series. Who else could they feature on that day? Bud Reth, executive producer of the show, mentioned Leslie Lemke. "Who's Leslie Lemke?" Jill Bishop, associate producer, asked.

Bud explained that his wife, Marcia, had seen Leslie sing and play the piano six months earlier at a community concert in Jackson, Wisconsin, a small town near Milwaukee. The auditorium had been packed, and Leslie had received a fantastic response. Marcia, a teacher of the handicapped, had come away highly impressed with this blind, retarded musician.

Reth drove out to Pewaukee to meet the Lemkes. As soon as Leslie touched the piano keys, Reth knew he wanted him for the show. His viewers would not forget this guest for a long time! He asked the Lemkes to appear on the final segment on Friday, June 13, 1980.

That was the morning Terry came for our interview and told me about the Lemkes. I had not seen the show, but later, when I began interviewing the Lemkes, I called the studio to ask if I could see a tape of the program.

A few days later I curled up in an overstuffed chair in a darkened room at the studio and watched the tape.

The studio audience consisted of children who had competed in Special Olympics. Terry interviewed four handicapped children who had won medals in several different events. They squirmed in their places, fought off their shyness, and managed to speak a few sentences and answer a question or two.

There was a remote from the *Milwaukee Citizens* office, and more commercials; then at last Terry introduced the Lemkes.

Once again May talked about how she had worked with Leslie, her faith in Jesus Christ, and the miracle. Then Leslie played: the Tchaikovsky first, then "Hello, Dolly" and "Everything Is Beautiful"—all the crowd pleasers.

Terry had been right when she described the show. Emotions ran high. People were wiping away tears; the children sat transfixed. Terry's mouth was trembling and her eyes were full. Meanwhile Leslie played on, his spastic fingers flying over the keyboard, his powerful voice overflowing the studio.

People looked as if they were watching an illusion. Whoever heard of a boy, unable to walk by himself, barely able to talk, performing like that? But Leslie was no illusion. He was human, he was playing, and he was in control. No wonder everybody was crying. They'd been talking about the handicapped all week, and suddenly, here was Leslie, a severely retarded youngster who is brilliantly gifted. His very existence was uplifting.

The audience was almost as smitten with the tiny, elf-like lady who was hopping around, calling out to the children and telling fabulous stories about this remarkable son of hers who could sing and play anything he heard.

The appearance was the Lemkes' first on Milwaukee television, and according to the phone calls and letters that followed, they were clearly a hit.

The series won the Public Awareness Award in November of 1980 from the Association for Retarded

Citizens in Milwaukee County. Five months later, in April of 1981, the station received a second honor, Media of the Year, from the State Association for Retarded Citizens.

Terry Meeuwsen remembers the show well.

"People always seem to enjoy human interest features, but nothing we'd ever done had received attention or prompted a response like that of Leslie Lemke's appearance on our show. We were still receiving phone calls from viewers weeks later."

In dozens of different ways viewers described how they were moved by Leslie's appearance that Friday morning.

> What a beautiful testimonial to the indomitable spirit of a human being who was considered a vegetable and hopelessly retarded.

> I'm writing while I'm watching Leslie Lemke play the piano and sing. Thank you, Terry, for showing Milwaukee another miracle worker, May Lemke. Today is my thirty-ninth birthday, and no gift could make me happier than to have heard Leslie.

> Your program on June 13 was special!
> The Lemke family is special!
> And I feel special having had the opportunity to view such God-given talent!

> Friday's program on the Lemkes was the most touching thing I have ever seen on TV. If God places people on this earth to do His work, May Lemke has got to be one of them.

A few months later the *Milwaukee Journal* published its account of the Lemkes. The story was picked up by the Associated Press and appeared in newspapers all over the country. Letters and phone calls began arriving from Texas, New York, California, Hawaii, Utah, Tennessee, and dozens of other states. Some of them read as follows:

> This young man, in giving a private concert for his parents, is giving one of the few things he can give. But how beautiful it is! What beautiful people! What a beautiful story!

> Mother Teresa is my heroine and May Lemke is a close second!

> This loving, selfless woman has devoted her life to teaching a twenty-eight-year-old child whose eventual response might have been, in all probability, non-existent. Her rewards, in his special gift of music, are perhaps greater than the rest of us may ever know.

> Mrs. Lemke, your story brought joy to my life today. Your courage and love shine like a star.

And from an eleven-year-old boy:

> Dear Leslie,
> Mom saw the article in the newspaper and read it to me. It told that you can play anything you hear note per note on the piano.
> You see, I have cerebral palsy, too. I play the piano for Bible class and I play by ear, too. I am legally blind. I really like playing for people. I don't play classical music, but I play songs like Four Leaf Clover, Five Foot Two, Anniversary Walz [sic]. I also play Happy Birthday whenever there is a birthday celebration.
> I hope your Mom can read this to you.

Paul Harvey talked about the amazing Lemkes on his radio broadcast the following day. Local television stations hurried out to feature them on their evening news shows. And on December 19, 1980, Walter Cronkite introduced Leslie on his "CBS Evening News" with these words: "This is a season that celebrates a miracle, and this story belongs to the season. It's the story of a young man, a piano, and a miracle."

Leslie returned to Channel 4 and Terry Meeuwsen to tape a touching Christmas Eve special, "Leslie and Friends." It was a sentimental evening with Santa Claus, an audience of retarded children, music and dancing, a Christmas tree, and plenty of treats. The show was repeated on Christmas Day.

On January 18, 1981, the Lemkes were featured on a twenty-minute segment of the television show, "That's Incredible!" This was the show that, even more than Walter Cronkite's news broadcast, launched the Lemkes onto the national scene. "Of all the stories we've ever told," hostess Cathy Crosby said, "none has touched me as much as the Lemkes. Thank you, May."

The Lemkes discovered that taping a television segment is not quite like giving a concert. "It was a long, exhausting day," May remembers. "The camera crew came in the morning and didn't leave until nearly midnight. I was bringing out trays of cookies, nuts, bread, apples, pears, 7-Up, and candy all day!

"There were three or four cameramen and then a girl who asked all the questions. I don't know who she was. Well, they shifted furniture around, took pictures all over the house, told us to stand here, sit there, kneel over there. They even had cameras outside, pouring through the windows. It really was incredible!" May stops to chuckle at her pun. "We didn't get to bed until 2 A.M."

The show was beautifully, painstakingly, and tastefully done.

It began with close-ups of May feeding Leslie and talking about the tiny, helpless infant who was brought to her that day twenty-eight years ago. "I had a duty to do and I was going to do it, no matter what it cost me!" Then there were close-ups of Leslie, hands trembling as he lifted a glass of milk to his mouth with obvious effort.

Dr. Treffert gave a clear, concise explanation of savant syndrome; then May again. "I said to myself, 'This boy can't stand so I'm going to drag him around so he'll feel what I'm doing!'"

She talked about the piano and the miracle, then suddenly the room was filled with music: a magnificent concerto fashioned from the spastic fingers of that severely retarded boy. Incredible! With Leslie's music in the background, May told of falling on her knees, weeping and thanking God for the miracle. Leslie played on, reinforcing the reality and beauty of this miracle.

Next, May talked about the first time Leslie sang. Leslie confirmed that second miracle with a powerful rendition of "Everything Is Beautiful," followed by "You Light Up My Life."

Dr. Treffert was back then with another slant on the Lemke story: the incredible dedication of May Lemke—her love, concern, care, work, and patience—and the melding of the two circumstances—Leslie's disability with May's devotion.

May talked while Leslie sang a hymn in the background. "Leslie's gift is from God. It couldn't be from anywhere else. And I know that Jesus is going to do lots of things for Leslie."

Next was this exchange:

Interviewer: Leslie, what does music mean to you?
Leslie: Music means it's from the heart.
Interviewer: Does it mean love?
Leslie: Yes, love!
Interviewer: Show me with music what you mean by love.

Leslie sang "The Lord's Prayer" as the camera withdrew slowly from the tiny cottage. It was the end of the day and dark outside. A full moon glistened on the lake, and Leslie's rich, clear voice penetrated the stillness of the night.

May received an outpouring of mail following the program and another stack when the show was repeated three months later on April 27, 1981. She regrets that there was no way she could answer all the mail.

"I've been meaning to write a letter to 'That's Incredible!' and ask them to read it on the air. I wanted to say that I'm deeply grateful to all the people who sent the nice letters and that it's impossible for me to thank each one of them because I have too much to do with Leslie."

These are a few of the letters the Lemkes received:

It was such a pleasure to see Jesus Christ glorified on a television show. And He certainly was last night as Leslie Lemke sang and played "The Lord's Prayer."

I have never heard the "Our Father" sung so beautifully and with so much love and feeling. Leslie, you give handicapped people of the world courage and hope. When I get on my knees tonight, I will thank

God for smiling down on you and for reminding us through public television that He is always present in our lives.

I was so happy my whole family was home that night so my two sons, aged 14 and 19, could see that God is still performing miracles in this day and not only in Bible times. Please tell Leslie he plays heavenly and sings like an angel.

I've never been a particularly religious person, but after seeing Leslie's great talent and your great love, how can one not believe? It's people like you and families like yours that make this world a beautiful place to live.

Therese Martineau, a fourth grade religious education teacher in Dracut, Massachusetts, wrote that her class had been discussing handicapped people—how God chooses to give some people disabilities that they can't understand, but He also gives special gifts.

A few weeks later, most of the class saw Leslie Lemke on "That's Incredible!" They asked Mrs. Martineau if they could write letters to Leslie. Here are some of their thoughts, unedited:

It's amazing that you can play the piano when your handicapped. I heard you were on that's incredible and it is incredible. Your a real smart person.

We all have things we can do good and things we can do not so good. I play the clarinet good but I don't draw so good. I liked the story of your life. It makes me feel good.

I think you have many talents and I think you can increase them by yourself. I think you are the best piano player and singer in the world.

I admired your courage and enjoyed your singing and I loved the way you played the piano. You have a good mother and you should be glad to have her.

And from an eight-year-old boy to his mother after seeing Leslie on television: "Mom, if anything should ever happen to me, how could I give Leslie my eyes?"

Chapter 13

A Plea for Understanding

I was driving home from the Lemkes one afternoon when the thought struck me: What did I *really* know about mental retardation?

I had come to know Leslie Lemke, but what about all those other retarded people out there, the ones who don't sing or play the piano? What kind of lives do they lead? What do they feel? What is their future?

I called the Association for Retarded Citizens in Milwaukee County and was directed to John Wilberding, citizen advocacy coordinator. When I arrived a few days later for our appointment, John led me to a comfortable, freshly remodeled sitting room on the fourth floor of an old building in downtown Milwaukee.

About thirty years old, John proved to be a serious, no-nonsense activist, and his strong convictions filtered through our conversation loud and clear.

"Please don't refer to them as *the retarded*," he offered first off. "*Retarded* should be used as an adjective, never a noun. We're talking about people who just happen to have a particular characteristic: mental retardation. How can I look at any other aspect of that individual's personality if he's called a retardate?"

I'd never thought of that. I tried to recall my *Journal* story about Leslie Lemke. Had I used "retardate"? I couldn't remember. But I knew I'd be more careful next time.

Wilberding moved on. He objected to the notion that all retarded people are children. "Until seven years ago," he said, "the Association for Retarded Citizens was called the Association for Retarded Children. It took us twenty-five years to admit that retarded people are not children all their lives.

"Do you know," he said, "to this day, there are *children's* toys and *children's* pictures in our institutions and nursing homes? Naturally, the general public reacts to these people as children. Even parents of retarded children have difficulty changing their attitudes when their children become adults. They've been told consistently, often by our professionals, that their retarded children always will be children."

I thought of the dedication to my book that I had been mulling over. I had considered dedicating it "to Leslie Lemke, to my nephew, Mark Turcin, and to retarded children everywhere, who are indeed God's Special Children."

"I guess you wouldn't approve of that, would you?" I asked, knowing full well the answer.

A look of dismay came over his face. "Well, I guess you can dedicate it any way you wish, but besides the word 'children,' I object to 'special.' To me, 'special' has a note of condescension in it. The term suggests that this person needs to be cared for constantly.

Now, how can I see this person as a functioning human being with abilities, potential, and feelings if I'm calling him one of 'God's Special Children'?"

"But 'special' can mean favored, too. It can mean something positive," I ventured. After all, I had a stake in this.

"You're right, it can. But I like to get people in the mainstream to concentrate on their likenesses, not their differences. I don't like seeing them singled out as people to be pitied. But remember, these are only my opinions. Professionals don't agree on everything. Some support things like the Special Olympics; others don't."

I was beginning to enjoy the exchange. Wilberding might be a few years ahead of his time, but he was making me think. And that was exactly why I had come.

"Are you ready for more?" He sensed that I was sifting through his ideas, thinking them over.

"I'm ready," I said quickly. "Tell me, are there more of these myths and misconceptions? I'd like to hear about them."

"Fine. Let's start with 'mental age.' A retarded person may be thirty-five years old, but people ask, 'How old is he *really?*' If that person reads and writes at, say, a five-year-old level, it is assumed he will be five years old all of his life. But what about the thirty-five years of experience that person has? If he's lived that long, then he has the feelings and emotions of a thirty-five-year-old. He's not likely to remain at a five-year-old level emotionally if he is encouraged to progress and is challenged to be independent. Retarded people learn more slowly, of course, but they can continue to learn for all their lives. They don't stand still."

"You know," I said, "I think I've always had a tendency to lock them in, to assume that academically, maybe even emotionally, they were standing in cement. They didn't move. I never thought of them as having the same needs that I have: to grow, to learn, to change."

Equally annoying to Wilberding is the assumption that retarded people are dangerous. He pointed out that this error stems from the fact that so many of them are institutionalized.

"It goes like this," he said. "Most communities have a place somewhere, probably hidden out in the middle of a cornfield, where they put their retarded persons. The only other people who live like that are prisoners. And we all know prisoners have committed a crime and are dangerous.

"But retarded people have never committed a crime. They are in no way dangerous. Yet, they are incarcerated, where they don't need to be and don't want to be. In most cases, they could develop, grow, and contribute to society by being allowed to live in our communities. I find that pretty heavy discrimination."

I was beginning to be convinced. Obviously, there are misconceptions. And problems. "How then," I asked, "are attitudes changed if we're all so caught up in the myths?"

"Not by speeches and media coverage," he said. "I can spend a month talking with groups, discussing problems, answering questions, and suggesting solutions. I doubt that my efforts change more than one or two people in any one group.

"But if we have contact with a mentally retarded person, if we make an attempt to get to know him as a person, then our attitudes begin to change.

"There's a group home for retarded people across the street from where I live. When the idea was proposed, the neighbors were scared to death of it. Now, five years later, they have seen that the home is not a detriment. It has not ruined our neighborhood. It's an accepted part of our community. Neighbors have come to know these people. I could have talked about acceptance forever with little effect. People had to experience it and see for themselves. Now the attitudes have changed, and changed favorably."

Group homes. A fairly new concept in the area of mental retardation. The idea has stirred plenty of controversy around the Milwaukee area in the past couple of years, but I had read little about it.

"Those are only for the mildly affected, aren't they?" I guessed.

"Absolutely false," Wilberding asserted.

He pointed out that a number of people in group homes were diagnosed as severely retarded at one time. But given an opportunity to *do* something, rather than to sit around all day, their functioning ability can change dramatically. He added that eighty to ninety percent of the retarded population is only mildly retarded.

Before moving to Wisconsin, Wilberding, who was then single, worked in a group home in Michigan for seven and a half years. Half the people in that home were diagnosed as severely retarded, but they were able to do almost everything for themselves.

Sixteen people lived in Wilberding's household and everyone of them participated in the ongoing functions of the home. "Of course, we had problems," he said. "I don't know of any group of seventeen people living together who don't have problems. But we learned to work things out, and that's important. We must always keep in mind that these are individuals, just as your own children are individuals. There are those who learn to function more quickly than others. Some cook more easily, some learn to clean more easily. We all have our own areas of expertise."

Don't we all function better in a home, where we are free to make our own decisions and have some control over our lives? I shuddered at the thought of living in an institution and having my life regulated by other people. *How we prize our freedom,* I thought to myself.

"Another thing," Wilberding continued. "It seems to me the goal of some institutions is to keep people quiet and their emotions under control. In truth, many parents with a retarded child at home operate the same way. They walk around on eggshells so their retarded son or daughter won't get upset.

"But they allow their other children to get upset. Why the difference? A person who can't get mad, can't really be happy. He's just somewhere in the middle all the time, unable to experience the joy of living. This is another advantage of group homes. Retarded people are allowed to express their emotions. They cry, they laugh, they get angry. They aren't living in an emotional limbo."

Sometime earlier, I had seen a reference to a sheltered apartment. "Is that something like a group home?" I inquired.

"Somewhat, but it's even less restrictive. The apartment usually consists of five or ten units. Two people live together in each unit, and there is one apartment manager. This manager also provides whatever support the other residents need: assistance in budgeting money, advice on a personal problem, whatever. Ultimately, some retarded adults are able to move through the whole process: from an institution to a group home to a sheltered apartment and finally, to complete independence."

I discovered that community acceptance of retarded citizens varies greatly from state to state. Allegan County, Michigan, for example, with a population of one hundred thousand has forty-four group homes. Milwaukee County, on the other hand, with a population of one million, has twelve group homes. Other states like Nebraska now have people living in sheltered apartments who, only ten years ago, were expected to live out their entire lives in institutions.

"How about getting jobs?" I asked. "Does the resistance found in neighborhoods exist in the workplace?"

"Of course it does," Wilberding said emphatically. "That's why we've set up sheltered workshops." He acknowledged that some retarded adults need such workshops because they can't meet the expectations of competitive employment. But he added that many *can* grow and move on to a competitive job *if* given the opportunity.

"I suspect there are fewer and fewer jobs available to them," I observed. "After all, our society continues to become more complex."

"You're right. Mentally retarded people were probably better off in rural America, before farming became so mechanized. In an agrarian society, there
was much more of a demand for unskilled tasks and
farming jobs, where these people fit in more easily.
As jobs have become more sophisticated, people who
are the least able to keep up with technological
changes stand out even more."

"What about young retarded adults leaving home
when they're between eighteen and twenty like their
brothers and sisters?" I had visited a couple who had
recently found a group home for their eighteen-year-
old retarded daughter. Mary was reluctant and fearful of leaving home at first, but after a few months in
the group home, she began to blossom.

"The decision was not easy," Patrick and Marge
Healy said when I talked with them. "We worried
that Mary would not make friends and that she'd feel
rejected by us. But we found an excellent group home
where there were four men and four women with
two wonderful people in charge. After Mary adjusted
to her new situation, people who know her marveled
at how independent she had become. Now, she and
her friends go shopping, take short trips, picnics, all
the things that young people do. Two of the people
who worked with Mary were married recently, and
Mary was even in the wedding!"

Wilberding agreed that many young retarded
adults do grow more when they're away from home,
as Mary did. "But parents have a hard time with that.
It's scary to let go of a person whom you see as not
being capable of fending for himself."

I decided to look into the cost differential between

institutionalized care and group homes. Figures published in April of 1981 by the Association for Retarded Citizens in Wisconsin showed a significant difference.

The average cost of institutionalized care in Wisconsin runs at least $80 a day, and up to $36,000 a year in some cases. Estimates go as high as $2 million for a lifetime of care. Nursing homes, by contrast, cost approximately $45 to $60 a day.

But group homes cost almost half that figure, around $30 a day. A foster home is closer to $20 per day and a sheltered apartment may cost as little as $10 to $15 a day. Those living in sheltered apartments also are likely to be gainfully employed, paying taxes and contributing to the economy.

Aside from the social and financial considerations, Wilberding is concerned about the human potential of this vast group of citizens.

"Leslie Lemke is an example of what is happening to a number of people who are retarded. They don't possess Leslie's spectacular single ability, but at the same time, they are proving they have abilities people never saw before. They can live more independently and be an integral part of society.

"For some people, success may be learning to ride a bus alone. That's no big deal for most of us, but for a retarded person, it means overcoming a huge obstacle and succeeding against the odds."

Getting past the condition. Seeing that person for who he is. I tried to assimilate all I had learned on my way home.

When I first met Leslie, I saw only his handicaps: his blindness, the palsy, his lack of response. I was so caught up in his disabilities I forgot he had thoughts and emotions—yes, even that he was a person.

But May wasn't so blind. So often, in those early days of our friendship, I talked only to May since Leslie didn't seem to understand. And over and over again she prompted, "Ask Leslie some questions. That's the only way he'll learn to talk."

I still see Leslie's handicaps, but I don't think much about them. I have learned to take his hand or put my arm around him to warn him when I'm going to plant a kiss on his cheek after a successful concert.

I know what he can handle conversationally, and I encourage him by asking questions. "How was your concert last night, Leslie?" or, "Hey, you've got a beard today!" or "By the way, Leslie, do you know Rachmaninoff's Prelude in G Minor? If not, you've got to learn it."

I suppose I didn't realize what was happening at the time. But I did what Wilberding was talking about. I got past the handicaps and discovered Leslie Lemke is, indeed, a person. He is funny, intriguing, a wonderful ambassador for Christ, and clearly one of the most gifted musicians I have ever heard.

Chapter 14

The Lemkes, Today

"How did you ever do it?"

I must have asked the Lemkes that question a dozen times, and I always received the same answer. I guess I couldn't bring myself to believe it, because I kept asking.

"Joe and I are different from other people," May said again and again. "We just accept things when God puts them before us. It's like accepting what you have to do in life. Things come at you and you don't say, 'Am I going to do it?' You say, 'Now, how am I going to do it?'

"I had been working for the rich all my life, taking care of their children. I thought to myself, 'Why not help this little one who has nobody?' "

Joe soon chimed in with his own philosophy. "I believe that our lives are all laid out ahead of us. Whatever God wants us to do, we just do it. We took Leslie and did the best we could with him."

I accepted that for a few weeks; then I was back at them again.

"But May, you had to be lonely! You got away twice in twenty-nine years—once for surgery and once when you went to England for three weeks. You *had* to get frustrated!"

May was never defensive, only amused. "Frustrated? I'm never frustrated! I just said to Jesus, 'This is what You have given me. I'm going to stick to it all my life until You tell me when to stop. I am Your servant, and I am happy to do the work You've put before me.' "

I don't know what I was after. I guess I wanted May to tell me that she pulled her hair and pounded the walls and screamed a lot. Maybe because that's what I would have done. But May never did.

Once, I used the word *struggle* in reference to her years with Leslie.

"Struggle?" May winced at the word. "It was no struggle. We were learning so much beautiful love all those years with Leslie. Our house is filled with it. And people see it when they come to visit. Loving someone is never a struggle."

May was right, of course. You do feel love in the Lemkes' house. Love, acceptance, humor, friendship—a refreshing place to visit. The credos are relax; take me like I am; say it like it is; this is the way God made me so why should I try to be any different?

Another revelation came when I began to arrange interviews with people who had known the Lemkes over the years: attorney James Ward, social worker Paul Baumgartener, Stance Bergelin, Dr. Treffert.

"The Lemkes? Oh sure, I'd be happy to see you. Wonderful family! It's about time people found out what May and Joe have done all these years!"

I didn't have to wonder if they'd see me. I didn't have to explain *why* I was writing a book. I didn't have to worry about breaking the ice. I was accepted. I was on the team!

"The biggest miracle," Baumgartener said one day in his office, "is that those three ever got together. They totally complement each other. May is so gregarious, so determined—which is why she was able to do all those things with Leslie. Then there is Joe, who is such a gentle, quiet man, perfectly willing to stay in the background. Yet he's a fine, fine gentleman and a strong support for May and Leslie.

"I sometimes wonder," he said thoughtfully, "what would have happened to this young man if he had ended up at an institution and if he had never had access to a piano. I wonder if he even would have lived."

He told me about the first time he heard of the Lemkes. When Leslie turned eighteen, May called the Waukesha County Department of Social Services to see if he might be eligible for some kind of aid.

"They sent me out to the Lemkes, and it just blew my mind!" said Baumgartener. "Here was this boy who couldn't even talk to me (he kind of grunted at that time); yet he sat down at the piano and played like a professional pianist. I'm a weekend musician, so I could see right away that he was making key changes as if he were reading the music. He had fantastic timing. He was doing things that only a professional musician would do.

"When May told me she had been caring for this boy for eighteen years and had never received any aid, I was dumbfounded! She said they had expected

him to die and when she called for help, she never
seemed to get anywhere. I immediately signed Leslie
up for SSI (Social Supplemental Income), and she's
been getting help ever since.''

Another topic frequently discussed in interviews
was the change in Leslie over the years.

''When I first met Leslie, I asked him questions and
he just sat there, like someone had turned off the
switch,'' Bergelin recalled. ''But when I call the
Lemkes now, sometimes Leslie and I converse a little
over the phone. If I'm giving May a message, I'll
often hear him responding in the background.''

Baumgartener, too, has noticed that Leslie seems to
be developing socially since his visit ten years ago. ''I
think he's beginning to relate to people and to be
more cognizant of who they are. When I talk to May
on the phone, she'll ask, 'Leslie, who am I talking to?'
and he'll say 'Mr. Baumgartener' very distinctly.''

I thought of the many interviews I had conducted
with May. When she couldn't think of a song or a
person's name or some small fact, she asked Leslie to
refresh her memory.

Sometimes, when the taping was long, Leslie grew
impatient waiting for us to finish and called out,
''Honey-love, I'm not shaved yet.'' Everytime, May
answered calmly, ''That will come later, love, when
you've had your bath.''

Then there was the first time I heard Leslie laugh. I
had taken an editor to meet the Lemkes. A bit of a
musician himself, the editor sang a duet with Leslie,
tried some harmonizing, and then played a composi-
tion he remembered from years back. The song was
not extremely difficult, and when the editor chal-

lenged Leslie to repeat it, Leslie laughed out loud. I was so startled that I cried out, "May, Leslie's laughing! I've never heard him laugh before!" Leslie proceeded to repeat the piece with a great deal of embellishment, and of course, the performance was beautiful.

May's concern for Leslie's health does not go unnoticed by her associates. She never accommodates anyone if she thinks it might be too much for Leslie.

One photographer on assignment tried to schedule a four o'clock appointment, to be followed by more pictures at Leslie's evening concert. He was coming from Chicago and didn't want to sit around several hours between the home shots and the concert. But May was adamant. "If you want pictures of Leslie, you'll have to come at one o'clock because he always rests a few hours before his concerts."

Baumgartener laughed when I told him the story. "That is very typical of May. Everybody else can wait, but Leslie comes first! And I think that's neat. I can remember when Leslie first started to give those little concerts. May called me on the phone to tell me where they were going and she was so pleased, so excited. But when the demands grew, she was truly concerned about his health. She called to ask, 'Do you think it will be too much for Leslie?' She will never accommodate people at Leslie's expense. She's very protective and very caring about him."

As the Lemkes' reputation grew and I became more involved with them, people asked me, "What is May Lemke really like?" I realized I hardly knew where to begin.

I told them that she can be extremely funny and a

little outrageous—like the time she and Joe took a nostalgic trip to England in 1958. May insisted on taking a picture of a Palace Guard before they left London, and she was determined to make him laugh.

The Palace Guards parade before Buckingham Palace and are one of London's most popular tourist attractions. They are not allowed to smile or laugh on duty.

Despite royal edict, May couldn't resist. She kneeled on the ground with her camera, poked her head under the huge iron gate, and whispered very loudly, "Hey, we're leaving for America in a few days. Nobody here will see the picture. So come on, have a laugh! I promise I'll keep it to myself."

She kept on and on, peering like a gamine under the gate until he started to smile. May snapped the picture as everyone around her laughed and clamored for the negative.

"Oh, I couldn't do that," May said. "I wouldn't want this boy to be in trouble. They might chop his head off or put him in a bloody tower for the rest of his life!"

May has changed little since the day she broke up the Palace Guard.

A call came one day from an Alabama man who had seen the Lemkes on national television. He had relatives in Wisconsin and wished to visit the Lemkes on his next trip. "Where can I find you?" he asked.

"Well," May explained, "just go outside and look under the bushes and you'll find a big rock. Lift up the rock and if a little leprechaun runs out, that's me!"

During a concert for physicians, she pointed to her

own doctor. "You see that doctor over there?" she asked the audience. "You know what he did? He messed up my stomach and I've been eating nuts ever since. I think he made me into a squirrel!"

The doctor jumped up and shot back, "I don't know what we did to you, but it sure seems to be working!" By then everyone was breaking up.

"Those doctors need to laugh," May observed casually. "Their work is so serious, being around sick people all the time."

May is perfectly capable of anger as well as humor, particularly concerning any injustice to Leslie. She let out her fury once following a concert at a nursing home.

"One of the clergymen gave Leslie a glass of wine," she recalled. "I don't even let him have soda water. I was so mad I don't even remember what I said. Leslie's never had a drink in his life. I really got after that man. What did he think he was doing, giving a retarded boy wine!"

Honesty is another strong Lemke characteristic. No pretensions, no facades.

When a call came from California asking if May, Joe, and Leslie would appear on the "Pat Boone Easter Seal Telethon," May's first response was, "Well, we're no fancy dressers or anything like that, you know. We're just plain people."

Another time she said, "I don't bother much about money, food, or clothes. I don't eat much and if I need something to wear, I just find a couple remnants and sew them together."

The Lemkes rely on friends and volunteers for transportation to and from their concerts. "We've never had a car and we never intend to get one" is how May phrased it. "We've gotten along fine without a car and a lot of other things that people think they need. So if they want us, they have to come and get us, whether by car, plane, or UFO!"

May Lemke is even a bit of a psychologist. Books have been written about guilt and anxiety, but she needs only one paragraph to set folks straight.

"I tell people, 'When you're older, you must start doing something to get those negative, burdensome things out of your mind. We all know there are sad things that happen. But you need to throw them to one side. There are other things for you to do. That's the only way to get them out of your mind."

Another amazing aspect of May's personality is her total inability to be intimidated. Producers, editors, entertainers, cameramen are all treated the same, usually with a bear hug and a warm welcome. "Just pretend you're renting this little cottage and make yourself at home," she says. "Do you want an apple—or some nuts?"

A high-powered New York producer discovered May's imperturbability during a television taping session. He was scheduled to film a short segment on the Lemkes following the taping of a local half-hour show before an audience of retarded children. When the local show was finally taped, the producer tried to get May's attention in order to proceed with his own segment.

"If you would just stand over there between Leslie and the piano . . ." he began, but May was already occupied. She was leaning over a little girl in a wheelchair who apparently had been abandoned by her escort.

"Nobody's taking care of this little girl," May said to the producer. "I wonder if you would bring her a hamburger, some fries, and something to drink?"

The producer simply did as he was told. When he returned with her order, May spread everything out on the little girl's lap, opened the can of soda, and *then* walked over and stood between Leslie and the piano.

At Leslie's concerts, May quits being the teacher and delights in his music with everyone else. But at home in the tiny closed-in porch, she is often the critic. "You're bumping too much, love. You're getting an exaggerated bumping."

Or sometimes it's the volume. "You're singing too loud, love. You'll have to calm down a bit. We're not in a concert hall, you know. Softly now, love."

"He's used to such big rooms," she explains. "He doesn't need a microphone because he's such a powerful singer. When he's too loud, this little room just vibrates!"

Frequently, she comments on her size, particularly during concerts.

"I may be only four and a half feet tall, but I feel like a giant. And remember, you tall ones have to look down all the time but I'm lucky. I'm always looking up!"

When she speaks of children, the joking and frivolity disappear, particularly when she talks about the handicapped.

"There's nothing wrong with retarded children," she says. "They've got better manners than we've got. When I talk to other children, I say, 'Take hold of their hands. You're not any different from them. They may even be more clever than you are. Listen to what they have to say and talk to them. Jesus loves all children, no matter what they're like.' "

Then there's her own faith: strong, persistent, indestructible. "When I first got Leslie, I was asking God for so many things. I didn't do anything without getting down on my knees and praying about it. And I've always gotten my answer. I believe that God can make miracles. And I believe that God wanted Leslie to grow up into something. So one day He looked down at him and said, 'Well, I think it's time we did something with Leslie.' *Sure*, we believe in miracles, don't we, Leslie?"

May's pride is not reserved for Leslie; it spills over for her whole family. Frequently, she talks about them at concerts.

"You know, I came over here all alone, just a young girl with nobody at all. But now I've got five children, three boys who each spent seven years in the armed services and two girls who grew up to become nurses. I've got a grandson who was an Honor Guard for President Ford and another who won a Purple Heart in Vietnam. All of my children are married, and I have nineteen grandchildren and ten great-grandchildren and everyone of them is lovely. Now, wouldn't you say I've done my bit for America?"

May's daughter Mary lives on a hundred-acre farm in northern Wisconsin. She has been designated Leslie's legal guardian after the Lemkes can no longer care for him.

"We have a river going through the farm, lots of pine trees, and a big house," Mary says. "I'd even like to take in a few other disabled or elderly people someday. They could fish, plant a garden—maybe we'll even have a swimming pool. We'll continue Leslie's concerts as long as he enjoys giving them. We all love Leslie. He's a part of all of us because he's such a part of Mother. He'll always have a home."

May's daughters can't say enough about their mother.

"She is everything good," Pat, her other daughter, says. "She's terribly generous. If someone is in need, she'll drop everything to help them. She sacrificed a lot for her children. We always came first.

"She is also very religious, very strict. When we were growing up, we got her messages over the dinner table—the importance of honesty, of not being prejudiced, of always being ourselves. We called them her 'little sermons.' But everything I believe today came from my mother. Those messages have stuck in my mind."

Mary echoes Pat's sentiments, adding a few of her own.

"Mother has always been a simple, uncomplicated person. One good lesson I learned from her was how to economize. We heard 'Waste not, want not,' and 'A penny saved is a penny earned,' over and over as we grew up. She was fabulous at making ends meet, using every little thing, never wasting anything.

"There were a few words that just weren't in my mother's vocabulary. One was *can't*. There wasn't a thing that my mother wouldn't try. She never used a recipe. Yet she is a fantastic cook. She always had an enormous garden full of huge, beautiful vegetables. One year she and Pat canned one thousand quarts of fruits and vegetables. She is a hard worker with boundless energy.

"She is also very creative. Besides making up her

own recipes, she designed her own clothes. She never used a pattern or a sewing machine. She just laid out the fabric, drew the pieces, cut them out, and sewed them up by hand. If she bought anything, she changed it so much you'd never recognize it."

Another word that May avoids is *sick*. Mary recalls the only time her mother was in the hospital for a major operation. She had a large portion of her stomach removed about seventeen years ago.

"She came out of intensive care and was supposed to stay for two more weeks," Mary says. "Instead, she announced that she was leaving. She could hardly stand up. I pleaded with her. 'You know, Mother,' I said, 'God does provide doctors to care for us.' "

"There is no doctor for me but Jesus Christ," May told her daughter. "The rest is up to Him. He can heal too, you know."

May's doctor said, "Well, you can't stop the English when they've made up their minds. She's going to go, and I can't stop her."

So May went home. She refused to go in the house until she had pulled herself along the fence for a few minutes, taking deep gulps of the fresh, crisp air. Then she asked Mary to fix her a pot of hot tea with a little milk and no sugar and some dry toast. After that, she went to bed and slept until the next morning. By then, she was ready to hop on the bus and run a few errands. She never went back to the doctor.

"What do you like most about your grandmother?" I asked Pat's daughter.

Without a moment's hesitation, she answered, "She's not afraid to be involved. She's fast to defend another's rights. She says exactly what she feels and never worries about what anyone thinks.

"My favorite story about Grandma is how she spoke out to the lady at the bank who pulled her little girl away from Leslie.

"Grandma was carrying Leslie when a little girl three or four years old walked over and reached up to touch him. The little girl's mother yanked her away as if he was a leper. Grandma was furious!

" 'You ought to be ashamed of yourself,' she said to the girl's mother. Everybody in the bank was listening, but Grandma didn't care. 'You have just robbed your child of a beautiful experience. Your little girl has got the love of Jesus in her, and you're making something rotten out of it. She's wanting to share with someone, wanting to touch a helpless baby, and you are pulling her away. When a child shows love, you should let that love grow. You should encourage it, not squash it!'

"Whenever I see an old person or a disabled person now, I remember that story. I make sure that I always smile or speak to them—I don't care how old or handicapped they are. I'm never afraid to touch them or take their hand or hug them. I always think of what Grandma would do."

Life has changed significantly for the Lemkes since that day in the bank so many years ago. Letters, telephone calls, and requests for appearances continue to flow in almost daily. James Ward, the Lemkes' attorney, handles their affairs and watches over their interests. A movie contract is being considered.

On October 29 1981, the Wisconsin Federation of the Council for Exceptional Children will present to

May the May Lemke Council for Exceptional Children Special Service Award. After this year's presentation, the award will be given annually to some person who has given special service to handicapped children.

But then again, life with the Lemkes really hasn't changed. Joe usually can be found out in the yard somewhere, chopping wood, or over at a neighbor's, helping out with some chore. Leslie most likely is sitting in his favorite chair, listening to a new record. But you know he'd like nothing better than to play a few songs before you leave.

May hasn't changed either. She still flies around the house, trying to keep her life in order, wondering when they're going to get the porch painted and would I like a few "pineys" to take home?

One pleasant afternoon—during my final interview with the Lemkes—May, Joe, and I were talking about Leslie's future. "What are you going to teach him next?" I asked.

"I'm trying to teach him to write his name," May said, "but so far he only scribbles. He does make a cross by himself, though. And I spell words to him. Of course, he never forgets those! He's changing and learning every day. We never know what's going to take place next."

Then she turned pensive and looked away for a moment. "Don't laugh at me, but I dream sometimes that Leslie will learn to play a concertina. Then he'll perform in a restaurant and walk among the people and play all the lovely songs they want to hear. Like they do in France."

How like May, I thought. *Nothing is impossible.* Suddenly I remembered my own dream. I'd almost forgotten it.

"Promise you won't laugh at me," I said. "I have a dream about Leslie, too. I dream that one day he'll play on the stage of a grand concert hall on a beautiful Steinway piano, accompanied by a magnificent orchestra."

"How lovely," she said, her eyes still far away.

I looked at my watch. It was time to go.

"May," I said, "if I asked you to describe Joe for my book, what would you say?"

"Oh, that he's a very good man." Joe slipped me a smile. "And he certainly is a good, hard worker. He's always out helping one of the neighbors. And he's very good-natured." She glanced at his old jeans, frayed shirt, and dirt-smudged face. "Well, sometimes he looks like a bum. Seems like he's always covered with dirt. But underneath, he's not a bum at all."

I looked at Joe. "Okay. Now it's your turn. What's so special about May?"

"Everything about her," he said casually.

"Oh, come on, Joe. What really stands out? One special quality."

"Everything about her," he repeated.

"But how about her funny sense of humor, or her cooking, or . . ."

Joe looked at me as if I were losing my hearing. "I like everything about May," he said softly.

Well, I know when to quit, I thought to myself. Besides, it's a rather nice tribute—to like everything. What more could you ask for?

I said good-bye. "Of course, we'll still see each

other!" *I've got to get out of here. I'm about to cry.* I knew they were standing at the door, watching me leave. I looked back one more time. They were both waving. I waved back.

I heard something and paused a second to listen. The music came from the porch, faintly, but there was no mistaking the tune. "Everything is beautiful," Leslie was singing, "in its own way."

Somehow, I never felt so close to Jesus. I hurried to the car, tears streaming down my face.